HEAVEN HERE

To Mary,

May God bless you richly.

—Josh [illegible]

IT'S CLOSER THAN YOU THINK

HEAVEN HERE

EXPERIENCE GOD'S GLORY
THIS SIDE OF ETERNITY

JOSH ADKINS

 All emphasis within Scripture quotations is the author's own. Please note that Destiny Image's publishing style capitalizes certain pronouns in Scripture that refer to the Father, Son, and Holy Spirit, and may differ from some publishers' styles. Take note that the name satan and related names are not capitalized. We choose not to acknowledge him, even to the point of violating grammatical rules.

DESTINY IMAGE® PUBLISHERS, INC.
P.O. Box 310, Shippensburg, PA 17257-0310
"Promoting Inspired Lives."

This book and all other Destiny Image and Destiny Image Fiction books are available at Christian bookstores and distributors worldwide.

Cover design: Twinkle Bhojwani

For more information on foreign distributors, call 717-532-3040.

Reach us on the Internet: www.destinyimage.com.

ISBN 13 TP: 978-0-7684-6178-7

ISBN 13 eBook: 978-0-7684-6179-4

ISBN 13 HC: 978-0-7684-6258-6

ISBN 13 LP: 978-0-7684-6257-9

For Worldwide Distribution, Printed in the U.S.A.

1 2 3 4 5 6 7 8 / 26 25 24 23 22

ACKNOWLEDGEMENTS

To my father, Mike Adkins, for your faithful life well-lived. Thank you for demonstrating integrity, fearing the Lord rather than men, handling money above reproach, and taking responsibility for your shortcomings. You are my hero!

To my mother, Carmel Adkins, for demonstrating repeated humility, compassion, and an unwavering belief in the Word of God. Without your faith and God's power, I'd not have been born. I love you!

To my sisters, Tricia and Tracy, for your loving support and willingness to do what is necessary to protect others. I'll never forget your caretaking and loyalty.

To my older brother, Andrew—thank you for cheering me on from the third heaven. I hope to make you proud!

To my Loft Church leaders and family, for your willingness to honor God's unusual choice in me as a pastor. Thank you for supporting me, encouraging me, correcting me, and honoring my leadership.

To my longtime friend, Dan Miner, for being the most loyal brother and servant leader I've known. Thank you for defending and sticking with me through good times and bad. Few know your uncompromising faith in the Lord despite heart-wrenching seasons and challenging circumstances, but I do! May Christ reward you to the utmost, my friend.

Thank you to Ben and Jodie Hughes for believing in me! Larry Sparks and Tina Pugh, thanks for your faith in me to represent Jesus and Destiny Image well. Carol Gardner, bless you for polishing this work. You are a saint!

CONTENTS

INTRODUCTION

"I've been talking to God for years, and He's not said anything to me yet!"

I was four years old when I offered that complaint to my mother. Chalk it up to the innocent musings of a child, but little has changed in my longings for authentic connection with the divine. I've never been satisfied with vague or distant expressions of God. I've always wanted to be near Him, to have real-time conversations and interactions with heaven. If God exists, and more aptly, if He is knowable, what else in this life could possibly trump the prospect of connecting with Him?

As I grew older, I began to adopt more mature understandings of a relationship with God. At least, that is what I believed them to be. That's what I was told—read a Scripture, wear your Sunday best, bow your head, talk to the sky, hope that the Man upstairs is listening, and if you do right enough, He just might receive you when you die. That's the gist of it.

Blind faith will do. Soldier on, boy, despite what soul-crushing disappointment in lack of discovery may lie beneath.

Like many, this was for some time my understanding of religious *being*. Although I grew up Christian, what little hope I had as a child for a blazing inferno of interaction with the living God was nearly snuffed out by the time I'd entered the angst of my latter teenage years. All that remained was a smoldering wick of evanescent hope in my religion.

That is, until I discovered the *more*. A heavenly kingdom-near had been hiding in plain sight, a spiritual reality that was both accessible and tangible. This connection would not only offer glimpses of God but would result in a supernatural adventure beyond my wildest dreams.

Now, let me be clear. I'm not speaking of the manifestation of any new-age philosophy. The principles, practices, and real-life miracles recounted in this work all expressly bow at the feet of Jesus. Still, if you are reading as someone presently outside of a Christian framework, I invite you to come along for the ride. I believe this book will offer compelling evidence for knowing a God you've previously considered unknowable. If you're reading this while already wearing some brand of Christian lens, it is my hope you will find inspiration to see God move in your own life in ways you hadn't thought possible.

This book is for all people—atheists, agnostics, non-Christian, or Christian—who've ever wondered if there is more to the search for significance through Deity. This is my offering to you as one man surrounded by an ever-increasing multitude who have discovered God can actually be known.

He *is* near. And while there is certainly much to be said of an afterlife, there is already a heaven here—and it's closer than you think!

> *For the kingdom of God is already among you* **(Luke 17:21 NLT).**

SECTION 1

AWAKENING

CHAPTER 1

THAT JUST HAPPENED

She was dressed in black. Straight-faced with eyes shut, it was as if the teenage girl not only expected to be disappointed but was already angered by my prayer.

It was a Tuesday night, and I'd just finished speaking to a weekly group of about 60 people in my loft apartment. After giving an invitation for salvation and personal ministry, the girl in black sheepishly made her way to the front. Her brother was a regular to our meetings and introduced us.

"This is my sister, and she wanted prayer," he said.

At first glance, I thought she was either a Catholic school girl, into '90s goth music, or a combination of both. From her boots to dyed hair, the only thing not draped in darkness on her body was the white neckline of her dress. To divert from the snap judgments I was likely wearing on my face, I quickly opened the conversation.

"So, this is your first time here?" I asked. She nodded in emotionless agreement. "I see. Glad to have you. How can I pray for you?"

"For several years, I've been struggling with an eating disorder," she said. "I'd like to be free from it, and anything else you feel God might say."

I told her that she was brave to confess her struggle, and that we'd gladly contend for healing. Laying my hand gently upon her shoulder, I began praying.

After a few moments, I peeked to see if God was doing anything. Nothing spectacular happening. After a few more words, I peeked again. The situation was the same. I clenched my eyes tighter now, hoping to conceal the doubts beginning to rise from beneath. I knew God loved this girl. Jesus gave His life for her. I knew the Holy Spirit wanted to speak despite any temporary awkwardness, so I silenced my mind as best I could and began to settle into a trust.

That's when I saw it. In a brief, passing moment, a picture of a daisy appeared in my mind. That's right, the white-petaled flower with a yellow center. There was nothing extraordinary about this flower, except, perhaps, its colors seemed especially vibrant. A single daisy. That was it; that was the impression.

"Now what, God?" I silently begged. "Can this really be You?"

The doubt I was experiencing wasn't merely from the vague imagery I'd seen, but also from the fact the girl standing before me seemed everything opposite of the "frilly" flowery type. I was afraid if I shared what I'd seen, she'd not just laugh. She'd thrust her goth-like arm directly into my chest, tear out my heart, and sacrifice it to the devil. Okay, that may be a little *Indiana Jones*, but honestly, I was scared of this girl.

Perfect love casts out fear though, right? I finally decided there was nothing to lose—besides my beating heart—so I stepped out on a limb. With my voice nervously cracking like a boy in puberty, I began relaying my spiritual impression.

"Umm...I see a daisy." Suddenly, more words began to flow naturally. "Yeah, I see a daisy over your heart. Its petals are bright white. I believe what God is saying is that while you may not see yourself as innocent—as daisies sometimes represent purity—He sees you that way because of His blood. He wants to wash your heart of all guilt and shame from the past."

To my shock, for the first time the girl began to smile. Then, tears welled up in her eyes. She replied, "I need to show you something."

She took her hand, reached up to that white lace collar and pulled it down a few inches. Just above her heart rested a solitary tattoo of a daisy, bright white petals with a yellow center. She went on to tell me it was the only tattoo on her body, and she had for a long while struggled with feeling like she'd lost her innocence.

Now, with boosted faith, I also began to prophesy that she was a heavy reader. "You're a bookworm, aren't you? I see you having two or three books on your nightstand that you're actively reading at the same time. In fact, it's almost as if your dream job would be to work in a library."

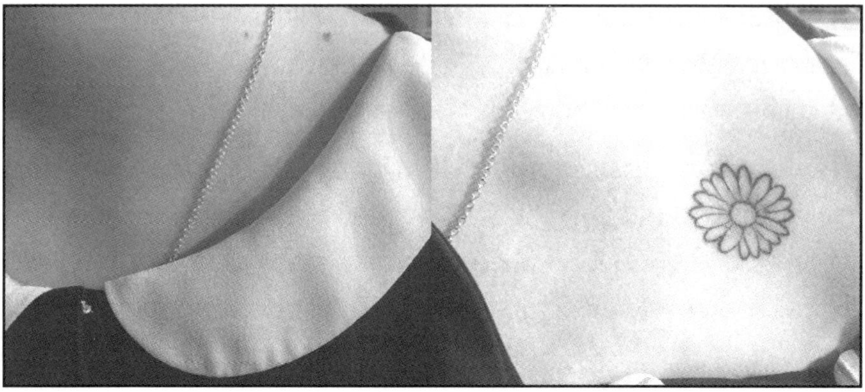

Now, both she and her brother were smiling at one another. She replied, "I am obsessed with reading, and am always in more than one book at a time. It's my favorite thing in the world!"

That moment shifted my life and ministry into a new realm of confidence. From that day forward, heaven seemed closer. God's voice became less of a mystery. I'd discovered many of those seemingly arbitrary internal impressions were not mere imagination, but divinely inspired! Hearing God would no longer be a sparse occurrence, but a regular event. Little did I know, this was merely the beginning of many more supernatural adventures.

CHAPTER 2

FATHER ESTRANGED

Like many in the west, I grew up in an ethos familiar with the cross of Christ. My father was an evangelist. God had opened doors for him and my mother to travel to many nations singing and sharing all Jesus had done in their lives. Through my parents I witnessed many beautiful depictions of God's faithfulness. I understood that He rewarded integrity and values. My father and mother were wonderful examples of these traits, and our family seemed blessed for it.

Amidst hundreds of these church services, both in my hometown and abroad, I'd also heard many messages about the sinful state of man. It was made clear we were a people in need of redemption. Without Jesus' merciful sacrifice, our depraved humanity would be doomed.

At four years old, I received Jesus as Savior and vowed to do my best to serve Him. However, as I grew older in my walk with God, I couldn't help but feel something was missing. "Yes, Jesus loves me," but if I were honest, God's love still seemed distant and impersonal. I knew my past sins had been forgiven at the cross. I knew my old life had been drowned in baptismal waters of forgetfulness. But what now? How do we walk out a life of obedience? What happens when we fail? After all He endured on the cross, what if we let Him down?

Although Jesus had once performed the most sacrificial act to redeem my eternal soul, I couldn't shake the feeling that God was still generally disappointed in me. I was a sinner saved by grace, after all. Only His merciful hand kept my wretched life suspended above the scorching lake of fire I deserved. At least that's what I'd been told.

This Is Growing Up

As a teenager I maintained a semblance of orderly Christian behavior. I didn't drink or smoke. I didn't do drugs. I rarely even attended parties. Instead, I made good grades, participated in extracurricular activities, student councils, and sports. My senior year of high school, I was nominated student president of Fellowship of Christian Athletes (FCA). All seemed well. I was the model Christian boy, on the outside anyway.

Truthfully, a cold war was waging within my soul. Secret lusts had crept in. Growing up during the advent of the internet didn't help matters. Various forms of pornography were readily accessible, and while I wasn't grossly immersed, I was not without such dabbling.

In addition, I was wrought with insecurities due to being a physically late bloomer. To add insult to injury, my closest friends all measured 6 feet 3 inches and above. They were dunking basketballs and taking the most popular girls to prom, while my slight, under-6-foot frame was still struggling to navigate puberty.

This adolescent disadvantage resulted in my attempt to compensate in other ways. I developed an acid tongue. I would brashly provoke peers to participate in rebellious acts of minor vandalism. In school I would sometimes verbally accost and subvert authorities I deemed incapable. At least, I put on a good show doing so in front of my peers. Later, I would cry tears of repentance at home. These behaviors, of course, were all emblematic of a simple desire to appear bigger than my body gave me credit for.

Like most teenage boys my age, I used to swim in pools and local lakes during humid summers. Oftentimes, someone would bring an inflatable beach ball into the water. I can remember trying to lay atop that ball to float. For a few moments, I could keep my weight balanced enough to hold it under. Sooner or later, though, the forces of nature would toss my frail body aside, and the ball would violently surface like a whale from the sea.

This summarized my young struggle with sin. Often lying in bed at night under conviction, I would think, "I will do better tomorrow." I rarely did. On days I felt I was outwardly doing okay, peace seemed attainable. On days I felt a moral failure, condemnation ruled my heart. Like the boy attempting to keep a buoyant ball beneath water, sin and shame would inevitably rise again.

This perpetual struggle to find peace and fulfillment eventually caused me to seek solace elsewhere. One day, while driving in my car, I heard a particular alternative rock song. Something about the music hooked me from the start. A few days later, I bought the artist's album from our local record store. I listened to that CD repeatedly, sometimes well into the early morning hours. Knowing I had musical talent running in my own family, an idea began to form.

Dreams of Stardom

I bought an electric guitar and spent hours teaching myself chords and leads. Eventually, I began to write my own music. For me, teenage hormones and the unsteady nature of high school dating relationships (or lack thereof) made lyrics and melody lines birth easily. I thought to myself, *If I can work hard enough to perfect my craft, I can make it out of this town. I might even become rich and famous. Then, I'd finally find peace and happiness.* Of course, I planned on appeasing my God-consciousness along the way by giving Christ credit for all my talent. That was *my* plan.

The summer before my senior year of high school, I found a few friends with similar musical dreams. We met in a small garage and began practicing for our school's upcoming talent show. We learned the songs backwards and forwards. When it came time, we stepped onto the stage and let it rip. To my shock, an entire audience of our usually caustic teenage peers rose to their feet and sang along. At the end of our short set, we received a lengthy standing ovation.

Something happened to me at that moment I'd never experienced before. Instead of the usual insecurity lurking beneath my awkward teenage body, euphoric feelings flooded me. I felt significant. I felt accepted. I felt loved.

After that night, all I wanted was to keep that high. So, we made our band official and began practicing religiously. We then recorded an EP and began touring, hoping to be discovered and "hit it big." Looking back, I realize how utterly foolish and cliché this all was, but I was young. I was another teenage kid looking for acceptance. I didn't realize the validation I sought could only come from the Father who was estranged from my heart.

Encounter with God

One day at the height of my musical pursuits, I had a life-changing encounter. I was driving down the road in my hometown, listening to music, not thinking a thing about God or religion. Suddenly, I heard a voice. It wasn't externally audible, but it was so internally evident, I pulled the car over in a parking lot to gather myself. I even turned around to make sure no one was hiding in my back seat. It was empty, yet I distinctly heard a voice beckon, "It's time you give Me 100 percent or nothing at all."

It was a surreal experience. Not only did I hear those words, but I could clearly identify the tone of the voice. It was authoritative, yet fatherly—loving, yet weighty, as if my response to its ultimatum would determine the course of my life.

I turned the key and shut off the engine. Looking up to heaven through my windshield, I sheepishly asked, "God, was that You?" I knew it wasn't me. I was in my right mind. I'd never heard voices before, and I had no reason to think such a notion. It was truly out of "left field." I spoke aloud by myself once more, "God, if that was You—and I'm pretty sure it was—what am I doing?" Suddenly, I had clarity.

"I know You're real, and I know You have a plan for my life, but I've been trying to do my own thing. So, if that was You, I'm asking You to take the desire out of me to do what I want to do, and instead replace it with what You want."

A few hours later, I drove home, shut the door to my bedroom and fell to my knees. "Jesus, I asked You to be my Savior as a young boy. I realize now, though, I have never truly submitted to You as Lord. I surrender everything to You. I give You all my plans. Take over my life, my career, my relationships, every part of my heart. I ask You to be in control of it all."

In that moment, spiritual scales fell from my eyes. I saw my selfish ambition for what it was—sin! God was real, He was alive, and all that ultimately mattered was knowing Him and His desires for my life.

Confirmation

Within days of this encounter, a fresh hunger for the Bible formed within my belly. To be honest, the Scriptures had for most of my life felt more a chore than a delight to read. I had a basic knowledge of the Bible's narrative, but my heart had not found the depth of value for the written Word that I have today.

After receiving Christ as Lord, I began to view the Bible as far more personal. Though there are a variety of literary styles, each with their own historical context, my spirit suddenly understood the Scriptures as living and active. They weren't distant historical texts, but God breathed merit into them for all generations. The Holy Spirit had revealed the Bible was personal to me! With that new viewpoint intact, I set off to read the Good Book cover to cover.

Now, nearly everyone in the world has heard of Moses. Most know the story of the Red Sea or the Ten Commandments. I certainly was no exception. But I'd never really studied his life beyond that. I was surprised to learn the books of Exodus, Numbers, and Deuteronomy had far more to say about his encounters with God than in dealing with Pharaoh's Egypt.

> *Thus the Lord used to speak to Moses face to face, just as a man speaks to his friend* **(Exodus 33:11).**

The first time I read the passage about God talking to Moses as a friend, I was deeply moved. I hungered for such a relationship. One morning, through tears, I prayed a bold prayer. I said to the Lord, "I want to know You like this. Whatever it takes, whatever You need to do in my heart to get me there, will You speak to me directly? I know we don't talk to literal arks (of covenant) anymore. But I want to hear Your Spirit clearly! Please!"

I'll never forget the response. That gentle, internal voice quickly becoming familiar whispered these words back, "If you'll learn My written Word first, I'll begin to speak to you more often like you're asking."

I'd never heard anything like that before. I couldn't think of a Scripture that stated those exact words. Still, there was a deep peace that came with the instruction. Besides, what harm could come from studying the Word of God? Still debating whether this impression was from God or my own mind, I walked to the kitchen to grab a bite to eat. At that time, I was about 20 years old and living at my parents' house during the summers between university semesters. My mother would sometimes spoil me by leaving a plate of leftover food in the refrigerator with cooking instructions written atop the cellophane covering.

After warming up one of these meals, I sat down in front of the living room television to eat. I picked up the remote and turned on the TV to two Christian ministers sitting across from one another at a table discussing the Bible.

Suddenly, one of the men said to the other, "When I got on fire for God, I wanted to know Him like Moses knew Him."

With the word I *seemingly* received from God moments earlier still fresh in my mind, I leaned in with increased interest.

The man then continued, "And the Lord told me, 'If you'll learn my written Word first, I'll begin speaking to you like I did to Moses.'"

A loud clanging came from my plate as the fork dropped from my hand. The man on television said word for word what the Holy Spirit had spoken to me in my bedroom only moments earlier. Not only that, but he said it in the same context of knowing God as Moses did! This seemed far too great a coincidence to ignore. I knew Jesus was confirming that I had not only heard His voice, but the message He'd given me was true. He wanted me to intensely study the Scripture. It would become a foundation and path to progressive communication with God.

From that day forward a true passion formed for Jesus. Deep in my bones, all I wanted was God, to know Him and make Him known. Not only had He set my spirit ablaze, but I knew beyond a doubt that He was calling me into a life of ministry. Before that could occur, however, He needed to reshape much of my understanding of Christianity. I needed to be stripped of all I thought I once knew about God the Father and allow Him to reintroduce me to His gospel, to Christ, and who I was in Him.

And that is precisely what He did.

CHAPTER 3

VERY GOOD NEWS

Therefore it says, "God opposes the proud but gives grace to the humble" **(James 4:6 ESV).**

The Bible is common in that everyone who reads it has access to the same information; however, the Bible is unique in that not everyone accesses the same revelation. Although the carnal mind can consume and retain information from worldly books, only the Holy Spirit can impart biblical revelation. Jesus declared, "He who has ears to hear, let him hear" (Matt. 11:15 NKJV). This *hearing* comes through grace and humbly reading to discover the relational heart of God.

As a young man, I understood Jesus had died on the cross because I was a sinner. My heart and life needed forgiveness. But something had always been missing. That missing part led me to perpetually struggle with sin and consequently to adopt a performance-based Christianity. God needed to open my hood and rework my entire Christian engine from the ground up. I needed a truer, deeper understanding of the gospel and of Him in general. In order to receive this overhaul, the Holy Spirit would take me back to the beginning, literally.

Genesis

Growing up in the Bible Belt, I'd heard the creation story. I could practically recite it. But had I really *heard* it?

> *Then God said, "Let Us make man in Our image, according to Our likeness; and let them rule over the fish of the sea and over the birds of the sky and over the cattle and over all the earth, and over every creeping thing that creeps on the earth." God created man in His own image, in the image of God He created him; male and female He created them* **(Genesis 1:26-27).**

In this passage, God introduces His first desires for mankind. Notice that in two verses, the word *image* is used three times—four if you include the synonym *likeness*. Now, when we read the rest of the Genesis account, we see God created light, water, and earth. He then created the sun, moon, and stars. After that, He planted trees, vegetation, crops; God ordained seasons of warmth, winter, seedtime, and harvest. He then created fish, birds, insects, reptiles, mammals, and every living creature upon the earth.

However, out of all of God's handiwork, from the vastness of space and time to the most microscopic organisms, He reserved His divine image for only one creation—human beings. No other object or entity had been given the privilege of being made in the likeness of God Almighty. We received that honor—you and I.

When I began to meditate on this simple truth, its implication became deeply profound within my heart. What an honor! How set apart we are! It's as if the Lord saved His best for last. But wait, there's more!

At the end of nearly each creation day, we read God pronounced a series of affirmations and blessings. Pleased with His handiwork, the God of excellence declared each design as "good."

> *And the earth brought forth vegetation...and God saw that it was good* **(Genesis 1:12).**
>
> *God made the beasts of the earth...and God saw that it was good* **(Genesis 1:25).**

The pattern continues. But what does God say after the creation of man?

> *God saw all that He had made, and behold, it was very good* **(Genesis 1:31).**

Did you catch that? God didn't just call us good. He needed another qualifier to describe the apex of His creation. Not until the invention of man did God use the phrase "very good." We are included in that qualification! We are the apple of His eye (see Ps. 17:8). We are the diamonds of His creation. God decreed from the foundation of the earth that you and I are *very* good!

Now, before any theologians reading lose their marbles, remember that sin had not yet been introduced. Rather, I'm speaking of the inherent value of humanity. The fall of man comes later, but it does come *later!* It's vital we highlight this truth. God was delighted to call us good. Why had I never noticed, let alone considered this?

One reason is that in an attempt to exalt Christ's supremacy, many preachers and teachers have historically demonized humanity. In fact, as a child I'd heard so much about man's depraved nature that I'd conflated the idea of sin's effects with my intrinsic value before God. Consequently, in not rightly dividing this issue, I'd developed a perverted understanding of our heavenly Father's nature. His true heart and demeanor had gone undiscovered in my heart.

Thus, my childhood understanding of the gospel was that an all-powerful, often grumpy God had arbitrarily made the decision to offer the humanity He disdained a ticket out of hell. After all, Paul did say he was wretched (see Rom. 7:24). Right? The problem is, that's not the beginning of the story, let alone the end! A man or woman may be saved by recognizing their sin and the atonement of Christ, but if we miss God's creation kiss—if we miss His acknowledgment of our value to His heart—we miss His true thoughts toward us!

Suddenly, I was seeing things differently. The Father not only loved me. He liked me! He celebrated my very existence. This revelation began reshaping my entire understanding of

Father God. He wasn't Jesus' angry Dad. The Father was actually the source of Christ's deep compassion. If Jesus wept, Father God must have that capacity too. In fact, before the flood, God demonstrated this very attribute toward a people who'd become so evil, they could no longer produce a single righteous thought!

> *The Lord was sorry that He had made man on the earth, and He was **grieved** in His heart* **(Genesis 6:6).**

See, in the fall, man hadn't lost his value. He lost his righteousness. Those are two entirely different things. My friend and fellow minister Justin Allen once put it like this: "The gospel of the kingdom is not about how dark and depraved and wicked the world is. It's about how good God is; it's about how God so loved this world!"

So, before we discuss sin and the fall of man, let's be clear, the Father's heart toward humanity has always been, and always will be, passionate love. From His point of view, we are not scum. We are not wretched in value. We are something worth dying for. In fact, the Father was willing to exchange heaven's best—Jesus—for us! In context of our intrinsic value, He calls us very good! Believe it.

Very Good Fruit

Today, we begin every discipleship school with this simple biblical teaching. It's been incredible to watch God unravel religious understandings and heal deep wounds as people receive the same revelation I did.

I'll never forget the very first time I taught this concept, an elderly man came forward immediately afterward with tears streaming down his face. He said, "I've been a Christian for over 40 years. In my 30s, I fell away from God and lived in homosexuality for nearly half of my life. It was my own doing, but it started after being hurt by the church. I was deceived into blaming God, believing He wasn't truly good. Jesus recently redeemed me, but what you taught today… if I had only known back then. This has truly changed my life. It unlocked something in me, even now. I'm so grateful for God's love!"

Countless others have since been touched by this simple return to the beginning of God's creation narrative. I'm more than grateful.

The Fall

So, what about the fall of man? To understand the nature of sin, death, and the fall of man, we should first look to the fall of satan. Though a controversial topic for some, our foundational beliefs about the devil influence our beliefs about the nature of the Father, creation, and humanity.

Many Old Testament passages are sprinkled with prophetic declaration and imagery. A Western, one-dimensional understanding of the Bible often misses this fact. Yet we see multi-dimensional scriptural realities in our Eastern ancestors' knowledge of prophecies regarding Christ. Jesus Himself referred to prophetic declarations about the Messiah embedded in Old Testament passages that our surface readings would have missed entirely. But in Hebrew culture, even the uneducated of the day were aware of their layered nature.

For example, today, and especially near each Christmas, many read the Isaiah 7:14 prophecy, "The virgin will conceive a child! She will give birth to a son and will call him Immanuel (which means 'God is with us')" (NLT) in reference to Mary the mother of Jesus of Nazareth. Rightfully so! Yet the fuller context of Isaiah 7:14 alludes to a more immediate fulfillment of a sign to Ahaz, then-present king, of God's Presence with Israel before its enemies. Most modern biblical scholars recognize this dual-natured provision. In *Commentary on the New Testament Use of the Old Testament*, Dr. G.K. Beale and Dr. D.A. Carson write the following:

> Although a handful of very conservative scholars insist on seeing solely a messianic prophecy here...most recognize that there is at least a provisional fulfillment in Isaiah's day, given the explicit statements of 7:15–16.[1]

Regarding satan's existence, similar dual-natured prophecies exist. A careful reading of Isaiah 14 and Ezekiel 28 reveals not merely a discussion regarding the literal king of Tyre, but an entity at work behind the scenes. This entity, referred to in

Latin as "lucifer" or in other translations as "morning star," was a former angelic being. That angelic being was the original creation state of the devil.

Some may suggest that God created satan as we know him to be the balancing force in the universe to God's good. Sort of the yin to God's yang idea. But this is not what Scripture reveals. The Bible tells us distinctly what God's created intent was for lucifer:

> *You were perfect in your ways from the day you were created, till iniquity was found in you* **(Ezekiel 28:15 NKJV).**

What a statement! "You *were* perfect." This upends many theories about the origins of evil and God's created intent. Not only have atheists tripped over this idea, but some Christians as well. So, how did iniquity enter a "perfect" satan?

I'd like to propose a tapestry of truth woven into the entire narrative of Scripture: Embedded within perfection is the nature of love—and true love demands choice. After all, forced love is no love at all. There is a different term for that—rape. God is not a divine rapist!

Like Adam, lucifer was created without sin. Only, he too had the same capacity to choose love or disobedience. He chose the latter. He chose envy of God's supreme reign over all creation. Lucifer said, "I will ascend above the heights of the clouds; I will make myself like the Most High" (Isa. 14:14). At this moment, iniquity was found in him. Sin corrupted his glorified nature. Lucifer then convinced some of the angels to rebel with him against Almighty God (see 2 Pet. 2). This is also why Jesus said, "I saw Satan fall like lightning from heaven" (Luke 10:18 NKJV). God cast him out. Sin's nature coursed through his being.

Now, where satan and the rest of the fallen angels resided between their fall from heaven and the temptation in the garden of Eden is unclear from our scriptural record. There's speculation among various theologians, but what is agreed upon is we then see a fallen satan in the garden speaking through the snake to Eve (see Gen. 3)

This narrative is imperative to viewing God rightly. The Father did not create an evil devil. He did not create a wretched Adam. God's plans and purposes were only good, perfect. It's just that in His wisdom, He knew in order to instill His nature of love within creation, choice would play an intrinsic part. Love demands choice, and with that ability to choose love comes the opportunity for sin.

The Law

Obviously, there are valuable lessons to be learned from the lives of Adam's first descendants. Early patriarchs such as Enoch, Noah, Abraham, Joseph, and more all comprise a heritage of faith which I will explore in further chapters. For the purpose of this discussion, though, it is vital to understand the law given to Israel through Moses, and how it prophetically buttresses the gospel.

The Scripture seems to offer three general reasons for the law being given. First, God set Israel apart from all nations of the earth through the law.

> *Now if you will obey me and keep my covenant, you will be my own special treasure from among all the peoples on earth* **(Exodus 19:5 NLT).**

Second, the law created a temporary means to commune with God. I say temporary because sin still held mankind in captivity from a spiritual level. Consequently, few could approach God's Presence and glory. Death would be the consequence if they were to do so inappropriately.

> *The Lord said to Moses, "Warn your brother, Aaron, not to enter the Most Holy Place behind the inner curtain whenever he chooses; if he does, he will die. For the Ark's cover—the place of atonement—is there, and I myself am present in the cloud above the atonement cover"* **(Leviticus 16:2 NLT).**

This warning was not given because God's heart was to kill. It was simply the nature of sin approaching the holy Presence of the Most High. Like oil and water, the two don't mix. The word *atone* in Hebrew means "to cover." The law then provided a system by which the chosen priests could approach God through temporary covering via the blood sacrifice of animals. However, the blood of bulls and goats could never fully cleanse and make alive the broken spirit of man (see Heb. 10:4). The shedding of natural blood merely provided a temporary means of "washing" in order that the nation may in small part commune with the living God. Thus, while the old covenant was holy, it was an incomplete solution for man.

This leads to the third substantial purpose for the law of Moses—to lead us to justification by faith in Christ. Paul lays it out in this way in Galatians:

> *Why the Law then? It was added because of transgressions, having been ordained through angels by the agency of a mediator, until the seed would come to whom the promise had been made. ... Is the Law then contrary to the promises of God? May it never be! For if a law had been given which was able to impart life, then righteousness would indeed have been based on law. But the Scripture has shut up everyone under sin, so that the promise by faith in Jesus Christ might be given to those who believe. But before faith came, we were kept in custody under the law, being shut up to the faith which was later to be revealed* **(Galatians 3:19-23).**

As if in a surprising plot-twist reveal, Paul tells us the ultimate purpose of the law was to bring an increased awareness of sin! This at first seems counterintuitive, but Paul goes on to reveal God's supreme wisdom and intent.

> *Therefore the Law has become our tutor to lead us to Christ, so that we may be justified by faith. But now that faith has come, we are no longer under a tutor. For you are all sons of God through faith in Christ Jesus* **(Galatians 3:24-26).**

In summary, Paul conveys that although the law was good from God's doing, it could not breathe life into the most inward part of man, the human spirit. That spirit had been broken, buried beneath the effects of sin and death since Adam's fall. Through the law of Moses, God desired to make evident that no matter how much effort a human being put into righteous behavior, he could never fix what lay beneath. The war in the very essence of the human heart required a peacemaker. Sin's deadly disease needed an antidote. Law couldn't do it. We needed something more—Some*one* more. We needed a Savior!

The Gospel

Enter Jesus Christ—our peacemaker, humanity's antidote for sin. He is the glorious Savior we needed!

Jesus did what no earthly man born under sin could do. He fulfilled the law! See, Jesus was born of a virgin for a reason. Although Adam is said to be part of Christ's lineage, God birthed Christ of His own heavenly bloodline. This immaculate conception allowed Christ to enter the world as clean, holy, untainted by the iniquities of Adam. Hence, Christ is sometimes referred to in the Scripture as *the second* or *last Adam.*

> *So also it is written, "The first man, Adam, became a living soul." The last Adam became a life-giving spirit* **(1 Corinthians 15:45).**

Adam came directly from God but fell to temptation. Since that time, all of humanity has suffered the crushing effects of his fall.

> *Therefore, just as through one man sin entered the world, and death through sin, and thus death spread to all men, because all sinned* **(Romans 5:12 NKJV).**

Christ, however, came as the second Adam born into the earth directly from God. In this, Jesus would have opportunity to do what Adam failed to do—live a holy life. In that holiness, He then was able to offer Himself as atonement for humanity. Jesus of Nazareth's untainted blood would enable Him to forgive sin's debt. His life of perfect obedience to the law qualified Him to become the one and only worthy mediator between God and man.

> *For as through the one man's* [Adam's] *disobedience the many were made sinners, even so through the obedience of the One* [Christ] *the many will be made righteous. The Law came in so that the transgression would increase; but where sin increased, grace abounded all the more, so that, as sin reigned in death, even so grace would reign through righteousness to enteral life through Jesus Christ our Lord* **(Romans 5:19-21).**

Understanding this backstory makes a difference in understanding the wisdom and glory of this gospel. Although the Father revealed man's intrinsic value in the garden, the impossible standard of the law's holiness revealed the inescapable depths of his brokenness. Righteousness by way of man's own doing was truly impossible—its holy walls too high for mere men to scale. We were doomed apart from Christ!

The fall and the law, when properly understood, create an awe for Jesus that ought to produce in us boundless depths of gratitude and worship. He truly is the only worthy One, the Hero of heroes, King of majesty beyond words. The *very* good news is this holy, ancient One thinks we were worth dying for! His passionate love for us from the beginning motivated Him to endure what no one else could—what no one else would!

Now, if all that were afforded in this gift were a ticket to heaven, it truly would be enough. But as the rest of this book will explore, that's only one facet of the redemption Jesus wrought. The kingdom of heaven is not merely a final destination. Christ is the door to an invisible kingdom to be encountered, explored, and utilized as a force against the enemy here on the earth.

If, after reading this far, you are sensing the conviction of the Holy Spirit, if you too see your need for a Savior, I want to give you the opportunity to meet Him right now! If you pray this prayer to God with sincerity, He will forgive your sins and wipe your slate clean by applying the precious blood of Jesus to your life. This is not the end of your journey with God, but the necessary beginning. Pray this after me:

> Father God, I acknowledge I'm a sinner in need of a Savior. I repent of my old life, living for myself. I ask You to atone for my sins with Your blood. Jesus,

I surrender to You completely as Lord. Save me! Come live inside of me. Make me a brand-new creation. Amen.

Congratulations, friend! If you prayed that with sincerity, the Bible declares you've just passed from death to life! You're born again, forgiven, saved. You are now a true Christian.

> *That if you confess with your mouth Jesus as Lord, and believe in your heart that God raised Him from the dead, you will be saved; for with the heart a person believes, resulting in righteousness, and with the mouth he confesses, resulting in salvation...for whoever will call on the name of the Lord will be saved* **(Romans 10:9-10,13).**

Whether you just started your salvation journey or have been walking with Christ for years, let's continue the exploration of this supernatural kingdom together. The depths of God are at our disposal and heaven is much closer than you think!

Note

1. G.K. Beale and D.A. Carson, *Commentary on the New Testament Use of the Old Testament* (Grand Rapids, MI: Baker Academic, 2007), 4.

CHAPTER 4

THIS CHANGES EVERYTHING

In my early 20s, I attended Murray State University in Kentucky. One day, while in line at Subway inside of our student center, I overheard a young couple in front of me talking about God. While pretending to look at the menu, I unavoidably eavesdropped on their conversation. The couple were openly angry about the fact a relative had invited them both to church. Disgusted with their perception of God, they brashly jeered and cursed Him.

My heart sank. I could feel the Holy Spirit grieving for their souls. I wanted to tell them about my wonderful experiences with this God they believed to be so monstrous. I wanted to share with them that Jesus was not only real, but He was good. But this was neither a church meeting nor Bible study. This was Subway. This line was for ordering turkey sandwiches, not hearing the spiritual exhortations of a second-year fellow undergraduate. *What would they think of me?* I shuddered.

If they insulted his grandmother, how much more might they berate a stranger for imposing his beliefs upon them?

I chickened out. I said nothing. I watched them pay for their food and walk away. After paying for my own meal, I dolefully footslogged back to my dorm. During that walk, I had an honest conversation with God.

With plastic sandwich bag in hand, I looked up to heaven and said, "Jesus, I'm a wimp for Your gospel. You have saved me and done beautiful things in my life, but I'm too fearful to tell people about You in public. I'm sorry. Please give me strength to share Your name."

After I got back to my room, I felt an urge to grab my Bible and spend some time alone with God. I withdrew to our dorm's study lounge. Once alone, I locked the door and opened to the book of Acts. I'd read Acts before, but this time, I wanted to particularly focus on how the first-century believers shared Jesus with strangers.

Nine chapters in, I reached the story of Saul of Tarsus (later known as Paul the Apostle) being knocked off his horse by a blinding vision of Jesus. Saul was then taken to a man's house in Damascus, where he did not eat or drink for three days.

A few hours later, Jesus appeared elsewhere to a man we might refer to today as an "everyday believer," a disciple named Ananias. Christ instructed Ananias to go to the house where Saul was staying and lay hands on him so that he might receive his sight and be filled with the Holy Spirit (see Acts 9:11-12). Having heard about Saul's reputation as an enemy of the church, Ananias humbly protested.

> *But Ananias answered, "Lord, I have heard from many about this man, how much harm he did to Your saints at Jerusalem; and here he has authority from the chief priests to bind all who call on Your name." But the Lord said to him, "Go, for he is a chosen instrument of Mine, to bear My name before the Gentiles and kings and the sons of Israel; for I will show him how much he must suffer for My name's sake"* **(Acts 9:13-16).**

What happened next in that dorm room study lounge, I had no more imagined happening than being asked to lead a space mission to Mars. I was in a tranquil and unassuming state. Yet immediately after reading Jesus' words to Ananias, I suddenly felt what I can only describe as a warm, tangible mist falling from above and onto the crown of my head.

I looked up to see if a heating vent was above me, or perhaps water was leaking from somewhere in the ceiling. Neither was the case, yet the warm sensation continued increasing in intensity. It traveled down my face, my neck, and eventually filled my chest. I looked around the empty room again for any possible natural explanation. There was none.

My hands began to shake. Then, my lungs began to fill with a unique sensation. What I can only describe as volumes of "liquid love" surged through my being. I was breathing so heavily an observer might think I was in distress, but the opposite was true. I was at peace. I felt accepted. A furious love from heaven had raptured my whole being.

Though I wanted to remain in that state of bliss forever, my natural mind and body seemed inadequate to house it. The love was too great. Something had to give.

I began weeping heavy tears. Deep sobs then turned to abounding laughter. In near convulsions of divine ecstasy, I raised my hands to God and surrendered. Suddenly, an unknown language burst from my mouth, foreign syllables flowed fluently from my tongue. For the next 45 minutes, supernatural power surged through my body to such a degree, I lost all inhibition. For the first time in my life, I could tangibly sense the living Presence of God, as if Jesus were standing right next to me.

I didn't know what to think or do with myself, so I stumbled outside to get some fresh air. When I entered the courtyard, the sun seemed brighter, colors more vibrant. I felt as though I were floating on a cloud. I know I must have looked crazy, but I walked around the perimeter of our dormitory, talking out loud to God. At one point, I exuberantly yelled, "I can literally feel You next to me, and nobody else knows You're here!"

That evening, I had to work a shift at our campus radio station. I'm not sure how I made it through the hours, mundanely announcing weather and the station ID during program breaks, but the Lord seemed to help. All I truly wanted was to get back to my room, pray, and read the Scripture.

By the next day, much of the tangible Presence had lifted, but something in me was different. I noticed a new measure of faith and boldness for the things of God. My fear of rejection had been eradicated. God had heard my turkey-sandwich prayer: "Lord, would You give me strength?" I didn't even realize what I'd asked for, yet I knew now what Jesus meant when He spoke these words:

> *But you will receive power when the Holy Spirit has come upon you; and you shall be My witnesses both in Jerusalem, and in all Judea and Samaria, and even to the remotest part of the earth* **(Acts 1:8).**

Something else astonishing occurred after this experience. When I prayed for other people, they would often encounter the same tangible Presence I had in that study lounge. Some I laid hands upon would even be so overcome, they'd fall backward onto the floor (see John 18:6). Others would shake, feel intense heat, or weep profusely in God's love. Still others would begin speaking in tongues for the first time—and it wasn't just those of Pentecostal or Charismatic persuasion. People of all denominational backgrounds would often encounter the Holy Spirit and speak in tongues after receiving my prayers! Even skeptics were touched!

> *But Jesus said, "Someone did touch Me, for I was aware that power had gone out of Me"* **(Luke 8:46).**
>
> *Then they* [Peter and John] *began laying their hands on them* [the Samaritans], *and they were receiving the Holy Spirit* **(Acts 8:17).**

First Steps into Ministry

That summer, I returned home and immediately began conducting Bible studies in my city. This was before social media, and I had no advertising, only prayer and word of mouth. Still, to my shock, a dozen youth and college-aged students came to my meetings. It was here I discovered the Lord had imparted another gift through my heavenly encounter—teaching.

When instructing from the Word of God, the youth would often comment how they could understand the Bible like they hadn't before. It would ignite their faith and passion for Jesus. In these meetings, God also began performing the first healing miracles I'd ever experienced. After receiving prayer, one girl who'd been medicated for manic depression burst into tears of joy. "I'm healed! I know it," she exclaimed. The next week, that same girl returned to report that for the first time in years, she'd had no symptoms of her long-standing condition. Beyond that, she'd thrown out her medication!

In those few summer weeks, several young people from my region were saved. Others returned to Christ in full repentance. I returned to college that fall more on fire for God than ever.

Then it happened. Some of my longstanding Christian friends did not understand my newfound fervor for the Lord. So, they politely distanced themselves. Others began to express feelings of distrust and disdain, believing I'd become too fanatical. For the first time in my Christian life, I experienced opposition from those within the church.

To help me find more like-minded peers, my former pastor back home, Dale Crall, informed me that Murray State University had a college campus ministry similar to his in Carbondale, Illinois. I looked up their information in the computer directory and decided to give their Wednesday night meeting in the student center a go.

The moment I walked into that first campus ministry meeting at Murray State, I sensed peace. Although the students with whom I was first shaking hands were strangers, they felt like home. It didn't take long to discover why. Many of these students had also been recently saved. Others spoke in tongues and had a particular zeal for evangelism.

Being with such like-minded believers pushed me to greater levels of boldness. At the suggestion of our campus pastor, I dove into apologetics (an intellectual defense of the Christian faith). I began preaching on benches near campus walkways. I often was head of the line to use evangelistic "surveys" with strangers on campus. These consistently bold efforts caused me to be recognized by the ministry's pastors. Soon after, I was offered a student leadership role. All seemed well, for a while anyway.

For nearly two years, I lived married to our ministry's mission to "win the world for Christ." I moved into a campus house with fellow leaders from the ministry. Alongside this move came increased responsibility to conduct and attend daily meetings and activities, including evangelism and missions outings. At the same time, I was still a college student. There were long hours of study, writing papers, and preparing presentations. In my music department, I had several midsemester and final performances to be judged by faculty. These were unusually stressful. Still, I gritted my teeth and did the necessary work.

However, this excessive pace of activity began to weigh heavily upon my heart. At first, I wrote weary feelings off as momentary lulls, something to just zealously push through. "I'll rest when I die," I brashly said. Soon, though, weary moments turned into mountains of exhaustion. I'd heard the phrase "burn out" a handful of times over the years, but always thought it was something only washed-up, undisciplined Christians experienced. I was wrong.

Eventually, I reached a point of being extremely busy with ministry activities while feeling incredibly distant from God Himself. I was seemingly doing all the right things but could no longer hear His voice or sense His Presence.

Seeking Remedy

Knowing something had to give, I decided to set aside a special time to fast and pray. Each day, I woke up while it was still dark outside and walked across campus to a small, isolated conference room in the student center. There, each morning, I sought God's face. I sat still. I worshiped. I prayed quietly. I prayed loudly. I prayed in tongues. I read the book of Psalms out loud. For two weeks, I poured all I had into God.

Bafflingly, during those two weeks, nothing happened. Zilch! The heavens seemed as painfully silent as ever. I was frustrated with myself. I was frustrated with God. I didn't understand His behavior. I was doing everything I could for Him, but He still wasn't answering me. I started to question if He even heard me to begin with. Had I disappointed Him? Had I lost favor in His sight? Was I even saved?

A few days after my fast, I had returned to my normal sleeping and eating schedule. I went about mundane, daily activities. I assumed I'd missed God, or perhaps even lost connection with Him for good. That is, until heaven surprised me.

Profound Truth

Three days after my fast, I was in my home studying when I developed a hankering for a snack. Suddenly, I remembered a particularly delectable item I'd purchased from the grocery store. My mouth watered. My stomach gurgled. I knew satisfaction was waiting for me in the old, paint-peeled kitchen cabinet. Keebler fudge sticks. You know the ones? Cheaply manufactured, overly processed wafers drenched in artificial fudge. An edible heaven on earth.

I walked from my bedroom to the kitchen planning to consume the whole box. I wasn't thinking a thing about God. There was no worship music playing—no "atmosphere" I'd cultivated for heaven to invade. Yet suddenly, a voice on the inside of me spoke so loudly, I nearly stopped to look behind to see if someone else was in the room.

The voice said, "I never asked My church to do anything for Me. I asked them to do everything *with* Me."

I was stunned. The sentence was so short, so succinct, and yet it pierced my heart. Revelation flooded my mind and soul. Suddenly I understood being part of God's church is not like working for a boss of a company. Working *for* a boss generally implies separation from him or her during duty. Bosses have their offices, we have ours. What we do *for* them aids the company as a whole, but their business is normally separate from ours. We are simply to measure up to our duty in the hope they'll approve. If we do well, perhaps they'll even throw a little extra reward our way.

This, unfortunately, is the way many Christians think about serving God. It's certainly how my heart had been postured toward Him. Although His power had become familiar in my life through the Holy Spirit, I still carried the idea that God was often far away, in an office somewhere in the sky, expecting me to "get her done." But now the Holy Spirit was explaining to me that I'd had the wrong mindset about ministry all along.

I wanted to be sure it was truly the voice of God, so I humbly requested the Holy Spirit prove Himself scripturally. "Lord, if that was You, would You give me Scripture to confirm this?" I asked. Immediately, several pertinent passages were brought to my memory.

> *And they went out and preached everywhere, while the Lord worked with them, and confirmed the word by the signs that followed* **(Mark 16:20).**

> *And working together with Him, we also urge you not to receive the grace of God in vain* **(2 Corinthians 6:1).**
>
> *God also testifying with them, both by signs and wonders and by various miracles and by gifts of the Holy Spirit according to His own will* **(Hebrews 2:4).**
>
> [The Greeks] *said to* [Jesus], *"What shall we do, so that we may work the works of God?" Jesus answered and said to them, "This is the work of God, that you believe in Him whom He has sent"* **(John 6:28-29).**

Wow! How could I have been blind to this before? While it's true we will be held accountable for how we've stewarded gifts and talents given to us, we were never called to steward them alone. We are invited to co-labor with our Management. Our Boss is actually always *in the room*. He still does the heavy lifting, but we are given the privilege of helping to facilitate His efforts. We are to work *with* Him, not for Him!

Could it really be that simple? That enjoyable?!

Of course, God wasn't discrediting prayer and evangelism. There were still healthy spiritual disciplines and good works to be done. Only, up to this point, I'd fueled these efforts through a sense of duty. Now, I was realizing God wanted that fuel to flow daily from a deep well of ongoing relationship and reception of love. He was teaching me that faith isn't trying harder; it's believing rightly. That faith comes by dwelling upon Christ's finished work (see Rom. 10:17; 12:2) and fellowshipping with the Holy Spirit (more on this in subsequent chapters).

Immediately, I applied this new paradigm to my life. The result was greater desire and stamina to pray, study, and evangelize. In fact, more people began to come to Christ than before! Instead of burning out in the process, I found a more continual flow of God's oil lubricating my revived heart. The great revivalist Smith Wigglesworth, known as one of the most fruitful ministers of the last few centuries, put it like this: "I can get more out of God by believing Him for one minute than I can by shouting at Him all night."

He's absolutely right. I have now lived in both mindsets and cultures, the abiding and the striving. One is like floating on your back in a rushing river. The other is like swimming as hard as you can against the current. The goal of both is the same, but the former yields far better results. You don't grow weary in the midst of it either. The fruit of resting in intimacy and Spirit-led obedience in the end always outdoes and outlasts striving.

> *For we who have believed enter that rest* **(Hebrews 4:3).**

In the weeks and months after hearing God speak these truths to me, I slept with a peace I hadn't in years—perhaps ever. One night, just before I closed my eyes, the Lord brought one more solidifying verse to mind.

> *I am the vine, you are the branches; he who abides in Me and I in him, he bears much fruit, but apart from Me you can do nothing* **(John 15:5).**

We accomplish *nothing* apart from Him! I saw it now. His job is to work through us. Our jobs are to simply abide! With tear-filled eyes, I looked up from my bed beyond the cheap, speckled ceiling of my campus house. My heart glimpsed into heaven as I gratefully whispered, "Thank You, Father. This changes everything!"

SECTION 2

REVELATION

CHAPTER 5

LIKE FATHER, LIKE SONS

Creator. Ancient of Days. King of kings. Lord of all.

Over the years, I'd become familiar with these attributes of God's nature. They gave me a deep reverence for Him. I feared the Lord. I desired to obey His commandments. Of course, these all remain true and noble heart postures and pursuits. However, this new shift from working *for* God to working *with* Him was continually taking me back to the drawing board. I was having to dismantle and rebuild some of my most basic ways of relating to Jesus.

In my early years of ministry, if you'd asked me if I were a "son of God," I would have answered, "Of course!" Truthfully though, beneath that seemingly tacit answer lies a very shallow understanding of sonship. I was much more familiar with being a servant of Christ. Being a bond-slave to Jesus is a privilege, after all. It carries with it an air of nobility. Humble is the man or woman who washes the feet of the King. Quite right. But Jesus was now pushing me beyond one-dimensional understandings of His nature and will. I needed another layer of foundation.

The Holy Spirit kept whispering, "Josh, serving is what you do; a son is who you are." At first, I kept asking myself, *What does He mean "who I am"?* God is infinite, sovereign, and holy! It's not about me; it's about Jesus! What then does it matter who *I* am?

Yet this was precisely the kind of human reasoning God needed to correct. Despite having good intentions, for years I had been living in a false humility about my identity in Christ. For most of my Christian life, I'd been told what I'd been saved from, but no one had ever really told me what I'd been saved *to!* Jesus needed to open my eyes more fully to His royal kingdom, and it was time for me to take ownership of its discovery.

Royal Sons

> *But to all who believed him and accepted him* [Christ], *he gave the right to become children of God* **(John 1:12 NLT).**

Throughout history, sons and daughters of kings have lived with privileges mere servants and subjects do not have.

First, princes and princesses normally abide in palaces, rather than outside their gates. This obvious proximity to their father's throne gives them special audience with him. Second, a king's sons and daughters are themselves considered royalty. They are highly esteemed, but not on merits of their own doing. Rather, they are born into royal rights established by their father and mother (or perhaps their ruling ancestors). In other words, one receives the benefits of another's labor.

These metaphors are not foreign to the gospel revealed in the New Testament. Jesus often spoke in parables using royal terminologies. The epistles are also littered with such language, sometimes even directly contrasting concepts of slavery and sonship.

> *So you are no longer a slave, but a son, and if a son, then an heir through God* **(Galatians 4:7 ESV).**
>
> *But you are a chosen people, a royal priesthood, a holy nation* **(1 Peter 2:9 NIV).**

If we've been adopted as royal sons, if we've been called heirs to God Himself, then we too live in close proximity to the King. Our home is the heavenly palace. We have been given a special audience with our Father!

> *Therefore let us draw near with confidence to the throne of grace, so that we may receive mercy and find grace to help in time of need* **(Hebrews 4:16).**

To boldly approach God is quite the proposal. For much of my life when reading that Scripture, my mind digested it, but my heart vomited it up. God is so holy, after all! How can we, mere humans, stand in His perfect Presence? Because the New Testament declares we are much more than mere humans!

One of the most popular phrases uttered in modern Christianity is, "I'm just a sinner saved by grace." I'm certain many reading this have heard it too. You may have even uttered these words yourself. It sounds humble. It seems pious. The problem is, it's untrue! Now, to be sure, we've all *been* (past tense) sinners needing the grace of Jesus. We didn't earn an ounce of God's forgiveness; our own righteousness before Christ is as filthy rags (see Isa. 64:6). But that's not where the story ends. So often, we neglect the progressive nature of God's salvation tale. Act II, so to speak, in His great epic declares the born-again believer no longer a slave to sin! In fact, the Bible goes even further in declaring born-again believers as *saints*.

How is this possible? How can we accept such titles of divine nobility while aware of our shortcomings? How can we reconcile God's judgments of sin alongside His declarations of sainthood over us?

A New Covenant

Many Christians still don't fully understand the new covenant. They believe we're under grace, but still a little law, just in case. This is because many don't grasp the full scope of grace itself. They think it's merely a pardon for sin. It's not. Grace is biblically defined as unmerited, supernatural empowerment to live righteously (see Tit. 2:11-12; 2 Cor. 12:9). It manifests outwardly when we inwardly believe in Jesus' work!

Paul told Timothy that the law is not for the righteous (in Christ), but for the unrighteous (see 1 Tim. 1:9). Is the law then evil? Surely not! God gave the law. It isn't bad news, it's just *old* news. As stated in a previous chapter, the law was merely a tutor to lead us to Christ. But once Christ came, faith replaced that tutor (see Gal. 3:22-25)! The writer of Hebrews reiterates this in stating:

> *When He said, "A new covenant," He has made the first obsolete. But whatever is becoming obsolete and growing old is ready to disappear* **(Hebrews 8:13).**

Paul also states:

> *For it is written that Abraham had two sons, one by the bondwoman and one by the free woman. But the son by the bondwoman was born according to the flesh, and the son by the free woman through the promise. ...So then, brethren, we are not children of a bondwoman, but of the free woman* **(Galatians 4:22-23,31).**

In Christ, ours is now a different law altogether (see James 1:25). It's imperative we understand that! We are under a new system of liberty and grace through faith. Moses' laws were fueled by fleshly works, but Christ's laws are empowered by spiritual love. This grace through love is so powerful, in fact, it can turn "do nots" into "want nots." In Christ, we don't lie or steal—not because we try to obey laws telling us "do not" but because it's loving to tell the truth. We don't honor our father and mother because tablets of stone say to do so, but because our renewed hearts compel us. That's God's desire for us under His new covenant.

You might say, "If it's the same result of obedience, why does it matter if it's by law or by love?" It matters because obedience to the law is only skin deep! You may avoid lying today, but when the heart remains unchanged, you will lie tomorrow. Paul goes so far as to say it this way: "the power of sin is the law " (1 Cor. 15:56).

When we live by the law, we set ourselves up for greater sin! See, the law wasn't designed to make us good; only Christ can do that. Sadly though, many Christians believe grace is still trying to obey the law of Moses, and just thanking Jesus for His blood when we fail. First, that wouldn't be grace. That would be mercy. Second, Jesus didn't just fulfill the law and forgive our sin, He *crucified* the law on the cross alongside our sin!

> *Having canceled out the certificate of debt consisting of decrees against us, which was hostile to us; and He has taken it out of the way, having nailed it to the cross* **(Colossians 2:14).**
>
> *For through the Law I died to the Law, so that I might live to God* **(Galatians 2:19).**

Besides this, if we fail to obey even one law of Moses at any point in our lives, we fail at the whole thing and come under its condemnation.

> *For whoever keeps the whole law and yet stumbles in one point, he has become guilty of all* **(James 2:10).**

That's a daunting reality! Under law, failure is inevitable and condemnation unavoidable. Such a person then lives up one day and down the next. His heart rides a perpetual roller coaster of emotion, with shame as the unavoidable destination. This is what Paul called being a "wretched man," a prisoner to the law of sin and death (see Rom. 7:23-24).

Wretched Is Wrong

Many misunderstand this context of Romans 7 and mistakenly attribute it to the new man under grace in Christ. They quote him declaring, "I do what I don't want to do" (see Rom. 7:15) as if to say, "See, even Paul couldn't help sinning!"

No! Paul was not saying he was still bound to sin in Christ. He was saying he was bound to sin apart from Him!

In the book of Romans, Paul is often laying out multi-chapter arguments to make his cases. This especially makes sense considering there were no chapter numbers when Paul wrote his letters to begin with. Those were added centuries later to simply help us better understand the topics and contents therein. Occasionally though, such appended divisions work against us. Micro-focusing on one chapter can at times lead to poor exegesis. We miss the bigger picture of what's being said.

If in Romans 7 Paul intended to declare we were still occasionally prisoners of sin, then he blatantly contradicted himself only moments earlier in Romans chapter 6.

> *Knowing this, that our old self was crucified with Him, in order that our body of sin might be done away with,* ***so that we would no longer be slaves to sin; for he who has died is freed from sin****. ... Sin shall not be master over you, for you are not under law but under grace...***and having been freed from sin***, you became slaves of righteousness. ...***But now having been freed from sin*** *and enslaved to God, you derive your benefit, resulting in sanctification, and the outcome, eternal life* **(Romans 6:6-7,14,18,22).**

These are definitive statements regarding our dead relationship to sin. Multiple times, Paul expressly says we've been freed from its power! Did you catch why? This is the crux of the matter—*because we are no longer under law, but under grace* (see Rom. 6:14).This is why Paul reiterates in First Corinthians 15:56: *"the power of sin is the law."* The two are inexorably connected.

So, if we are no longer under the law, we are no longer under the power of sin. Paul says instead we are now slaves to righteousness (see Rom 6:18). In modern vernacular, that's like saying, "I can't help but do right!" That may seem a radical shift in thinking for some, but it is the truth nonetheless! What if we woke up every morning with "I can't help but do right today" as our predominant thought? I'm not suggesting living in denial when we do sin—I'll address that in a moment—but what if every day, instead of hoping we didn't fall into sin, we instead expected to continually bump into righteousness? Indeed, that is precisely how we should believe!

> *For as he thinks within himself, so he is* **(Proverbs 23:7).**

What then of Romans 7? Let's look a little more precisely at the context:

> *For we know that the Law is spiritual, but I am of flesh, sold into bondage to sin. For what I am doing, I do not understand, for I am not practicing what I would like to do, but I am doing the very thing I hate* **(Romans 7:14-15).**

"I am of the flesh, sold into bondage to sin"? Does that sound like what we just read in chapter 6 when Paul says we are no longer slaves to sin, but to righteousness? No! Notice, Paul is talking about himself in relation to the law of Moses. Don't let his use of present tense language here trip you up. He's using it to speak rhetorically about himself before Christ. It's a literary device, not a doctrinal timestamp. He's preaching the predicament of attempting to live holy under law, setting us up once more for the need of grace!

> *For I joyfully concur with the law of God in the inner man, but I see a different law in the members of my body, waging war against the law of my mind and* ***making me a prisoner of the law of sin*** *which is in my members. Wretched man that I am!*

Who will set me free from the body of this death? **(Romans 7:22-24)**

Notice in verse 23, Paul uses the phrase *"making me a prisoner of the law of sin, which is in my members."* We've already seen this contradicted in Romans 6, but Paul gives the direct antidote to this moral imprisonment only three verses later!

> *For the law of the Spirit of life in* ***Christ Jesus has set you free from the law of sin*** *and of death* **(Romans 8:2).**

Do you see it? Under the law, Paul declares he *was* a prisoner of the law of sin, a wretched man. He wanted to do right, but something inside perpetually waged war against him, resulting in repeated failure. However, *now* the Spirit of life in Jesus has set him free from that very law of sin! Once again, he makes clear the law imprisons, while grace through faith in Christ makes free!

> *For what the Law could not do, weak as it was through the flesh, God did: sending His own Son in the likeness of sinful flesh and as an offering for sin* **(Romans 8:3).**

Many may be shocked to hear not a single passage in the New Testament addresses born-again believers as sinners by identity. Not one! The only passage one might contest concerns Paul calling himself "chief of sinners," but there again, the context is his former life. On the contrary, Christians are called *saints* 62 times in the New Testament!

For He rescued us from the domain of darkness, and transferred us to the kingdom of His beloved Son...He has now reconciled you in His fleshly body through death, in order to present you before Him holy and blameless and beyond reproach—if indeed you continue in the faith **(Colossians 1:13,22-23).**

Considering these truths, I'd like to propose that much of the church doesn't have a sin problem as much as they have a righteousness problem. They either don't know or don't believe they are new, holy creatures in Christ! This failure of faith results in many believers chronically struggling with self-worth, fear, worry, anxiety, depression, and more. In their hearts, they've not believed the righteous effects of the gospel, so they still live by what they do rather than what Christ did. That's like using Jesus as a crutch to keep walking on a broken leg. But Jesus isn't a crutch. He's a Great Physician. He not only heals our proverbial "broken leg" but gives us entirely new natures.

For indeed we have had good news preached to us, just as they also; but the word they heard did not profit them, because it was not united by faith in those who heard **(Hebrews 4:2).**

Blood Doesn't Cover

Another popular saying among even Christian preachers is, "God doesn't see you, He sees the blood of Jesus."

I understand the heart of the sentiment, but it leaves the suggestion we're still of loathing to God—that if not for His covering, He'd not be able to look upon us. That too is inaccurate! To the contrary, if we're born again in Christ, the blood of Jesus has cleansed us from all unrighteousness (see 1 John 1:9). Grace is not a covering of sin, but His underserved power to remove it. His blood is not a cloak to shield us from His sight, but a cleansing agent to redeem us to our God-intended, royal family status!

> *God made him who had no sin to be sin for us, so that in him we might become the righteousness of God* **(2 Corinthians 5:21 NIV).**

How is it possible that we could represent God's righteousness? It's because God actually killed the old you and me the moment we were born again in Christ. So then, He's not making an old you and me better. He can't work with those old natures at all, so instead He crucified and baptized them with Christ! He then raised brand-new creatures, ones He could put His *Holy* Spirit inside!

> *Or do you not know that all of us who have been baptized into Christ Jesus have been baptized into His death? Therefore we have been buried with Him through baptism into death, so that as Christ was raised from the dead through the glory of the Father, so we too might walk in newness of life* **(Romans 6:3-4).**

Don't Raise the Dead Man

How do we then reconcile the truth of the new, righteous creation within with continued moments of failure (sin)?

My heart leapt at the revelation of my new identity in Christ. It formed a necessary foundation for much I will share in the remainder of this book. Still, one question continued to plague me. Finally, I asked the Lord about it:

"God, I believe I am new, now called holy, righteous, and above reproach. But if this is true, why do I still sometimes sin?"

Two simultaneous truths emerged over the next few weeks as an answer to my question. The first came suddenly, only a few days after I initially prayed. I was in the shower when the Holy Spirit broke into my shampooing. His words were again succinct, yet deeply profound. In an almost coy way, the Spirit asked me, "Did I not give you power to raise the dead?"

My heart flooded with illumination. Normally, when I would think of resurrection, I would think in literal terms. Either it would apply to Jesus, those He and the apostles raised from the dead, or the desire within my own heart to see such miracles today. But this time, the Lord was using the word *resurrection* in a metaphysical context. A light bulb turned on.

The old or dead man is truly dead (see Rom. 6:2; Eph. 4:25). However, in Christ's kingdom, dead things can still be resurrected! Our old flesh may be six feet under, but it still has a voice. It still occasionally cries out from the grave, "Raise me, raise me!" But we don't have to. We mustn't allow our talking dead to become our walking dead!

By default, those in Christ live first by the Spirit. That's why we're called "slaves to righteousness" and not "strivers for righteousness." When we believe the truth about who we are, our first instincts are then spiritual. But when we sin, we are *choosing* to raise a dead man! We are putting grave clothes back on a new body they no longer fit. That's why for the believer sin brings such strong conviction! Its clothes feel awkward, itchy, and unfitting. Before Christ, we were chained to our dead man's desires. In Christ, however, we've been given supernatural power to leave him and his desires in the grave. That is, unless we've seared our consciences through rebellious acceptance of dead works (see 1 Tim. 4:2).

The key then is to remain in our default position of Christ-given victory by the renewal of our minds and regular fellowship with the Holy Spirit (see Rom. 12:2-3; Gal. 5:16). (I'll expound on fellowship with the Spirit a little later.) "Don't raise the dead man" may seem a "duh" command, but it unlocked for me a door that had previously held my soul captive. I no longer saw the reality of sin in a righteous believer as paradoxical, but instead a matter needing progressive revelation to remedy.

> *So then, brethren, we are under obligation, not to the flesh, to live according to the flesh—for if you are living according to the flesh, you must die; but if by the Spirit you are putting to death the deeds of the body, you will live* **(Romans 8:12-13).**

Now, I don't want to make light of sin and its destructive effects. Sin is the reason for Christ's suffering. He willfully chose to endure the cross because of His great love. Nevertheless, our sin fashioned the nails that pierced Him. So, we ought to hate it! I'm simply trying to detail ways in which the Word and Spirit offer escape from its entrapment.

What About Process?

The second truth the Lord showed me for remedying sin came in layers. Much can be found directly in Scripture. I'll attempt to briefly unpack it.

There seems a distinction within the Scripture between *willful* and *unwillful* sinning. All sin may technically be a choice, but not all choices are conscious decisions we make with omniscient awareness. Our spirits may be perfect (see Eph. 4:25-26), yet our souls are in process, pursuing what the Scripture refers to as sanctification (see 1 Thess. 4:3; Phil. 2:12). In other words, some parts of Christ's redemption in us are automatic. Other parts undergo a process.

It is the soul in process that often houses long-standing issues needing renewal and redemption before holiness can be achieved. This process includes the removal of strongholds, lies still sometimes believed via ignorance of an unrenewed mind. It can also involve the tweaking of flawed personality traits, emotional traumas and triggers, and even deliverance from demonic spirits. This is, of course, a broad topic of discussion. Some of the most brilliant fathers and theologians of the faith throughout centuries have written entire volumes on sanctification. Obviously then, I cannot satisfy the full breadth of knowledge and revelation on the subject in this book.

However, for this context and purpose, we'd do well to remember that while our souls are in process, Jesus is patient. He gladly participates in that process *with* us. In fact, I believe He's cheering us on! Some parts of our sanctifying journey can and should be traversed quickly, as we choose to judge ourselves honestly and exchange old patterns of thinking for God's truth. However, we are not called to live in a perpetually stressful state of introspection. For there are likely imperfections remaining within each of our souls that we've not yet even recognized, let alone eradicated through striving or self-flagellation. People nitpick others' faults. We even nitpick our own. But Christ nitpicks our strengths!

> *How precious are your thoughts about me, O God.*
> *They cannot be numbered!* **(Psalm 139:17 NLT)**

So, while we take this Christian walk seriously, we must keep in peace and joy amidst the journey (see Matt. 11:28; Rom. 14:17). Jesus looks at us with eyes of pride! He's always calling out our gold. The Father is the gardener of our souls (see John 15:1), and He knows how best to prune our imperfect (unconscious) parts.

Hope in Repentance

That said, there are other types of sin not brought about solely by unconscious flaws, but by conscious decisions.

The Bible seems to refer to these as *willful* sins. Rebellion can be the chief cause of this type and is a dangerous motivation to continue in (see Heb. 10:26-29). That is not to say that patterns of willful sins can't also in part be brought on by broken or unresolved matters within the soul. They certainly can, and that is why ministries of counseling, inner healing, and deliverance can be so beneficial, if founded in biblical truth and the Spirit's supernatural empowerment. I will touch on aspects of these ministries in subsequent chapters.

The purpose of writing this section is to bring hope. We should never justify sin, but we must realize when we as believers commit it, we have an Advocate well capable of cleansing and setting us back on a path of righteousness.

> *My little children, I am writing these things to you so that you may not sin. And if anyone sins, we have an Advocate with the Father, Jesus Christ the righteous* **(1 John 2:1).**

When we fail, we must not wallow in guilt. For we have not lost our positions as sons and daughters of God. He isn't kicking us out of the palace because we act up. Even disobedient sons are still sons. He may discipline us, but He disciplines those He loves (see Heb. 12:6). So long as we remain in Christ, He never strips our adoption or reduces us back to mere servants. We're in the royal family! So, if you've sinned, get back up and back in the Spirit. It is your right and inheritance as a son of the Holy One.

> *Though he* **[a righteous man]** *fall, he shall not be utterly cast down; for the Lord upholds him with His hand* **(Psalm 37:24 NKJV).**

Servanthood reminds us of who we humbly are not. Sonship reminds us of who we confidently are. Both are valid in their right place. In my journey, God never wanted me to abandon the heart of a servant, but He needed to shift my kingdom stance from mere defense to offense. In this, I began to discover I belonged to a much more vibrant, powerful family than I ever realized.

CHAPTER 6

BROTHERS IN ARMS

With a firmer grasp of sonship intact, let us move to another aspect of spiritual kinship—one I believe is rarely mentioned, let alone understood. Not only does God delight in calling us sons and daughters, but He also deemed us brothers of Jesus Himself!

> *For both He who sanctifies and those who are sanctified are all from one Father, for which reason He is not ashamed to call them brethren, saying, "I will proclaim Your name to My brethren"* **(Hebrews 2:11-12).**

At first, the term *brother* may seem a mere concession of a royal family dynamic, but indeed as I would soon discover in my journey, the implications of this word are far reaching. This divine brotherhood is another topic that could be greatly expanded, but for sake of brevity, I will simply draw out two main points.

A Brother to Us

You may have heard the Scripture, *"My ways are higher than your ways"* (Isa. 55:9). It's true, except once again, it's not the full story.

In order to relate to our humanity, Christ chose to leave behind His "higher" heavenly nature when coming to the earth. I'm not denying Christ was equally God and man. I subscribe to what theologians refer to as the "hypostatic union," or the combination of divine and human natures in the incarnation of Christ. However, within that mysterious union, Scripture makes clear that Christ did empty Himself of godly nature for purposes specially ordained by the Father. This shouldn't be controversial, if one merely rightly divides the matter in appropriate contexts.

> *Who, although He existed in the form of God, did not regard equality with God a thing to be grasped, but emptied Himself, taking the form of a bond-servant, and being made in the likeness of men* **(Philippians 2:6-7).**

One such context involves Christ's relation to temptation while upon the earth. If Jesus functioned in the fully manifested nature of His Deity, temptation would not be possible. For God cannot be tempted to sin (see James 1:13). If, however, He willfully laid aside that aspect of His nature for the purpose of relating to us as a brother, He would be thoroughly tempted as any human being.

> *For we do not have a high priest who cannot sympathize with our weaknesses, but One who has been tempted in all things as we are, yet without sin* **(Hebrews 4:15).**

Now, the writer of Hebrews connects Christ's high priestly role with His identity as our brother. As our high priest, Jesus fulfilled the law of Moses, not by divinely avoiding temptation, but by overcoming it through submission to the Father as an obedient Son. His aid in victory was the Holy Spirit that He might demonstrate our path to victory also!

In essence, Jesus says to us, "Brothers and sisters, as your older brother, I know what you are experiencing in the world. I have great compassion for you in your struggle against sin, because I've been there! But I overcame sin by the same Holy Spirit I've given to you, to demonstrate the way you may overcome also. Follow My lead!"

Again, if Jesus had achieved victory over sin merely because He was God, how could we ever expect to walk as He walked (see 1 John 2:6)? But Christ demonstrated this victory as an older brother to pioneer our path (see Rom. 8:29). In this, He became a high priest not merely for the purpose of sin's atonement, but as One who can sympathize and offer hope to us in our sufferings.

Brothers to Him

> *As the Father has sent Me, I also send you* **(John 20:21).**

A second effect of our brotherly love kinship to Jesus is that we are called to do the same works He did while on the earth. As an older Brother, He became our role model to follow!

Let me be clear: no one will ever be a Son in the way Christ is equal in Deity with the Father, nor could we offer similar atoning work for the sins of humanity. Christ stands alone in these regards. However, in terms of our relationship to the Father's kingdom being made manifest upon the earth, being a brother of Jesus reveals the Godhead's desire for us to continue the family business!

Why Jesus Came

What is that business? No true believer would deny Jesus' mission to seek and save the lost from sin (see Luke 19:10). Forgiveness of sins is the paramount purpose and effect of the gospel. However, the Bible teaches that it was not the totality of Christ's purpose on the earth. God has a broader vision, one some of the church has ignored, denied, or at times fought against.

Jesus came to institute a heavenly kingdom on earth. He came to restore all things.That process of restoration included destroying the works of the devil on the earth here and now.

> *The Son of God appeared for this purpose, to destroy the works of the devil* **(1 John 3:8).**

If Christ's mission were merely about forgiveness of sins, why did He preach about the kingdom of heaven being near? Moreover, why did He attach that proclamation to supernatural works?

> *"The kingdom of heaven is at hand." Heal the sick, raise the dead, cleanse the lepers, cast out demons* **(Matthew 10:7-8).**

One might argue healing, deliverance, resurrection, and various displays of the Holy Spirit's power were merely to demonstrate Christ's divinity—that He was proving His Messianic identity by the Father's works through Him. I would then ask, why give over 80 disciples authority to do the same supernatural works (see Matt. 10:1; Luke 10:1)? If the goal were merely Jesus' fame, why send miracle workers out to villages wholly *absent* of His personal Presence? Not to mention, after Christ's resurrection and ascension, why perform miracles through Peter, John, Stephen, Philip, Barnabas, Paul? The list goes on.

I believe the answer is: Jesus' mission was manifold. Forgiveness of sins, healing proofs, teaching insights, and feeding the poor are all truthful effects, but the broader mission of Christ was rescuing us from the kingdom of darkness and transferring us to the kingdom of light (see Col. 1:13).

> *To open their eyes so that they may turn from darkness to light and from the dominion of Satan to God, that they may receive forgiveness of sins and an inheritance among those who have been sanctified by faith in Me* **(Acts 26:18).**

So, if the *what* of Christ's mission was mass redemption, I'd submit to you the *why* was love. If love were the primary motivating factor of the Father in sending His Son (see John 3:16), then the works of Jesus were not merely to prove His Messianic identity, but to compassionately emancipate men and women from the cursed chains that bind (see Matt. 9:36).

> *Moved with compassion, Jesus stretched out His hand and touched him, and said to him, "I am willing; be cleansed"* **(Mark 1:41).**

Same Family, Same Mission

Love as God's motivation in miracles adds an entirely new dimension to Christianity. The question then isn't merely if Jesus did miraculous works to redeem and restore, but if we should also. And if we should, to what degree?

I believe one of the most overlooked character traits of God is His desire to share His work with humanity. Some would protest this notion, citing God's declaration, "I am the Lord...I will not share My glory with another" (see Isa. 42:8). Of course, that is the truth, but like all things, it has a context. In that passage, God is declaring He will not tolerate idolatry, His people worshiping other gods. If, however, we overgeneralize that passage to mean only Jesus was to do the works of God on the earth, we dismiss a massive amount of other Scripture declaring otherwise. In one such verse, Jesus blatantly states:

> *Truly, truly, I say to you, he who believes in Me, the works that I do, he will do also; and greater works than these he will do; because I go to the Father* **(John 14:12).**

After Jesus had spent three years "working the fields," He then told His brothers and sisters it was their turn. In effect, He said, "I'm going back to the Father now. So, tag, you're it!" Christ was the Father's ambassador on the earth. When He finished His "active duty," we then became the Father's ambassadors on the earth (see 2 Cor. 5:20).

Ambassador Duties

When ambassadors of the United States, for example, are sent to a territory or region, they've already been given a "green light" to act in certain ways on behalf of their leaders back home. They don't have to pick up the phone and passively ask permission for things they've *already* been charged to do. If they did, they'd likely be reprimanded and/or removed. No, ambassadors are sent to boldly *re*present the declared interests of their authorities.

So it is with us concerning the Father's already revealed will in the earth. Christ set our example. We must do as He did. We may ask permission from the Father in areas we've not been given clear directives, but as for the areas Christ demonstrated in His life, we are to presume our marching orders have not changed. In our mission, the Holy Spirit is our earpiece connection to the "home office." He may direct the *how* and *when* of those orders, but the *what* and *why* has already been made clear!

Authority of the Believer

In the garden, God delegated to man authority over the earth. When man gave in to temptation from the devil, however, that authority was made subject to sin, sickness, death, and the powers of darkness (see Rom. 6:16). In the gospels, we read an exchange between Jesus and the devil that further reveals the authority satan "inherited" from the sons of men.

> *And he* [the devil] *led Him* [Jesus] *up and showed Him all the kingdoms of the world in a moment of time. And the devil said to Him, "I will give You all this domain and its glory; for it has been handed over to me, and I give it to whomever I wish. Therefore if You worship before me, it shall all be Yours." Jesus answered him, "It is written, 'You shall worship the Lord your God and serve Him only'"* **(Luke 4:5-8).**

Notice, Jesus never contested the devil's claim to have been given dominion. To some degree, satan *did* legally hold that "claim" over men. That is, until Jesus arrived. Christ came to crush satan's head. During His ministry, Jesus walked in authority over the powers of sin, because He was without it. So, satan had no claim over Him. Jesus did as He and the

Father fully pleased regarding men. Jesus then taught and delegated authority to His disciples to do as He was doing. He gathered 12, and later 70 more to go into every town and village in Israel demonstrating the kingdom of God's redemptive work.

> *As you go, preach, saying, "The kingdom of heaven is at hand." Heal the sick, raise the dead, cleanse the lepers, cast out demons. Freely you received, freely give* **(Matthew 10:7-8).**
>
> *Whatever city you enter and they receive you, eat what is set before you; and heal those in it who are sick, and say to them, "The kingdom of God has come near to you"* **(Luke 10:8-9).**

Upon the disciples' return, Jesus further explains matters of authority:

> *Behold, I have given you authority to tread on serpents and scorpions, and over all the power of the enemy, and nothing will injure you* **(Luke 10:19).**

These instances, as powerful as they were, all took place *before* Christ's ultimate triumph. If Jesus had authority over the devil before His death, how much greater authority has He been given after laying down His life!? The cross of Jesus was the proverbial stake through the heart of darkness. Through His death and resurrection, Christ took back the keys of death and hell, setting free the captives both then, now, and forevermore (see Heb. 9:15).

And Jesus came up and spoke to them, saying, "All authority has been given to Me in heaven and on earth. Go therefore and make disciples of all the nations, baptizing them in the name of the Father and the Son and the Holy Spirit" **(Matthew 28:18).**

Notice after announcing His ultimate authority, Jesus immediately transitions to addressing our role in the earth. "Go therefore" is in reference to His authority and infers a transfer of delegated permission or authority to us. So then, we the church are now God's ambassadors in the earth (see 2 Cor. 5:20; Eph. 1:23). As little brothers and sisters of Christ, we've been given the consent of heaven to live, move, and minister as Jesus did. And what precisely did Jesus do?

- Seek the lost
- Love the hurting
- Heal the sick
- Cast out demons
- Raise the dead
- Bind up broken hearts
- Release peace and joy
- Feed the poor
- Teach and disciple nations
- Commission the next generation

These things and more are our family business. Accepting our royal positions as righteous children and siblings of our

King is not diminishing God's glory. On the contrary, it's more glorifying of Him, because as we abide with faith and confidence, He causes us to bear much fruit. We may never shed blood for the sins of the world, but we are called to reconcile them as our Holy Brother did! He is our example, because we have the same Father.

> *Jesus said to her, "...but go to My brethren and say to them, 'I ascend to My Father and your Father, and My God and your God'"* **(John 20:17).**

CHAPTER 7

THE UNVEILING

"It grew back!" she exclaimed.

An alarming phrase. So imprecise, so unspecific. So requiring of medical attention? Like a shark baited to chum in the water, I responded in the only way one instinctively could.

"What grew back?"

"My hymen!" she screamed.

Okay. Surely, no one in the history of civilization had started a conversation this way. Yet here we were, talking about a subject that would make most men uncomfortably shift in their seat, let alone a minister.

Thankfully, Lydia was my friend, a co-leader in ministry, and known for her purity. She had just returned from an annual checkup to the gynecologist. This would not normally be something she'd report to anyone about, but after hearing the fuller context of the story, I was astonished and grateful for her telling it.

Though Lydia was now a strong woman of God known for living a sexually pure lifestyle, that hadn't always been the case. In her early 20s, she'd gone through a failed marriage. Her ex-husband's adulterous affairs broke her heart and crushed her spirit. After the divorce, she felt lost, had numerous relationships, and was sexually active with men.

A few years later, she had a radical encounter with Jesus that changed her life. Her heart had been redeemed. Her physical virginity was gone, though, seemingly lost forever. That is, until after a bold prayer inspired by a revelation that had changed all our lives for the better in Christ. I'll finish this story a little later.

Divine Romance

From the book of Genesis through Revelation, the Song of Solomon and everywhere in between, the Bible uses marriage as an analogy for Christ and His church. In Genesis 2, the Bible says that when a man becomes of age, "a man shall leave his father and his mother, and be joined to his wife; and they shall become one flesh" (Gen. 2:24). What does this mean, "shall become one flesh"?

The Scripture is clear that individuals always retain an element of autonomy, even in marriage. Each is responsible for the stewarding of their hearts before God, how they honor others, their thinking, conduct of speech, etc. In other ways, though, God's design is that a married couple are recognized as one unified being, cleaving to one another. One translation of the word *cleave* in Hebrew is actually "to be glued together." Heaven and hell recognize this conjoining in unique and powerful ways.

For example, the apostle Peter states that a husband and wife walking in peace and mutual honor for one another are a powerful prayer force in the kingdom of God. When their unity is in dysfunction, however, the heavens can in many ways be closed off to them!

> *In the same way, you wives, be submissive to your own husbands.... You husbands in the same way, live with your wives in an understanding way... show her honor as a fellow heir of the grace of life, so that your prayers will not be hindered* **(1 Peter 3:1, 7).**

What a sobering reminder of the importance of unity! Another aspect of becoming *one flesh* obviously entails the sexual relationship between a husband and wife.

> *The king has brought me into his chambers* **(Song of Solomon 1:4).**

Now, the church at large is notorious for shying away from any discussion of sexuality. This is unfortunate, because while the devil certainly has his perversions, God created sex. The Holy, Sinless One invented it, not the devil. He imagined and fashioned every aspect, including the very anatomy of each gender's reproductive organs. Trouble comes only when we engage in God's sexual invention outside of the parameters He laid out for its safety and enjoyment.

Just as in the garden of Eden, the devil has tried to convince much of humanity that God's guidelines for sex within marriage are unnecessarily strict. Some might even pronounce His instruction as a "killjoy." After all, why would God give us such passion and then attempt to hinder the way in which we express it?

Before Adam and Eve ate from *the tree of the knowledge of good and evil*, they were safe, filled with joy and pleasures, and thrived in direct fellowship with the Almighty. Unfortunately, they soon discovered how costly listening to the lies of the serpent was! Enjoying that which God created outside of His guidelines literally killed them, not to mention doomed the rest of humanity, had it not been for Christ. The devil convinced the first man and woman God was withholding something good from them. In reality, God was protecting them from death! Today, the devil uses the same deceptive scheme regarding sexuality. But the God who created intimacy gave us guidelines for definite reasons, and He knows exactly what He's doing!

The most important reason God designed sex to remain inside of marriage is because He intended for it to glue two individuals together for life. What takes place in this consummation is not merely a temporary moment of mutually enjoyed pleasure. No, a covenant is also made—one of spirit, soul, and body.

Covenant

In many ancient cultures, sex between a new husband and wife was understood as being not merely the joining together of two lives, but that of two extended families. Throughout history, marriage has even brought warring tribes and nations into peace! The *covenant* made between a husband and wife often entailed protecting and caring for one another's families, to the degree that if another family or tribe were to go to war against the family of their new spouse, the other would be willing to defend them to the death. Thus, a covenant was a life contract between two parties, literally "till death do us part." For Israel, that covenant was recognized as being ratified by blood.

Ancient Jewish weddings often lasted many days. After enjoying initial festivities, the bride and groom would then enter their tent and bedchamber. However, unlike western weddings of today, these ancient families would not disperse and go to their homes. No, they would wait outside of the couple's tent for the consummation of their marriage to be made complete. The newlywed couple would then offer the blood-stained sheet from their bedchamber to the best man, throw it over a wall or line to display to the wedding guests that blood had indeed been spilled! Seven days of celebration would often ensue, ultimately culminating in the "marriage supper," as both families celebrated the covenant between them made official.[1]

Holy Hymen

Blood is essential to covenants because God declares life itself is in the blood (see Lev. 17:11). The Lord created the human body with purpose. While sin, death, and the enemy sometimes war against our physical bodies on this earth, nothing of God's intended design is in vain. Every aspect is fearfully and wonderfully made (see Ps. 139:14).

In a woman's anatomy, the hymen is a thin membrane, a *veil*, typically crescent-shaped, that stretches across some or all the vaginal opening. As of this writing, most evolutionary biologists and physicians still have no definite understanding of the hymen's purpose. They are baffled by it. God isn't though. He created all things with unique purpose and intent, and some mysteries are only revealed in Christ.

Now, occasionally a young woman's hymen may accidentally rupture during vigorous exercise or some other physical trauma. In most cases though, this delicate part of a woman's anatomy remains intact until the very first time she engages in sexual intercourse. And what happens when that hymen breaks? Blood is spilled. God embedded a physical sign of marriage covenant within the female anatomy itself. This is why a woman's virginity is precious and holy in the sight of God. It's why the Lord intends for her blood to spill with one man, in an act of consummation. That blood is the ratifying substance of the covenant. It is holy. But that's only part of the story!

Since the creation of the tabernacle during the time of Moses, and in every temple the Israelites constructed since, a veil separated God's manifest Presence from man. For centuries, only the high priest could enter the innermost chamber of the temple, the Holy of Holies. Before entering, he was required to engage in a myriad of ceremonial washings and cleansing, lest he die in the Lord's mighty Presence. One man, once a year would enter to make atonement for the sins of the people with the blood of bulls and goats. As discussed in previous chapters, this was a temporary solution, finite in scope and effect, though necessary until Christ's more perfect sacrifice would come.

The book of John records that the moment Jesus died on the cross, the veil in the temple of God was violently torn from top to bottom (see Matt. 27:51). When Jesus shed His blood, the veil that separated God from men rent, and for the first time in human history since the fall of Adam, all men who would enter through Christ's blood could become intimate with God!

Do you see it? When Christ willingly spilled His blood, He unveiled Himself, so you and I could forever become intimate with Him!

> *By a new and living way which He inaugurated for us through the veil, that is, His flesh* **(Hebrews 10:20).**

Religious men may consider this an offensive analogy, but Christ often offends the religious! It is to be considered in absolute holiness and purity of heart. Remember, God created these things, including His frequent use of the bridal union as a metaphor for Christ and the church!

> *Then he said to me, "Write, 'Blessed are those who are invited to the marriage supper of the Lamb'"* **(Revelation 19:9).**
>
> *For your husband is your Maker, whose name is the Lord of hosts; and your Redeemer is the Holy One of Israel, who is called the God of all the earth* **(Isaiah 54:5).**

When I first considered this new understanding, it gave me a deeper reverence for Christ, His sacrifice, and even my own sexual purity! I'm still a virgin while writing this, but after receiving greater revelation of these things, I had an even higher respect for the sanctity of marriage and its bed. I asked God for further confirmation to let me know He was in this, and wow, did He respond!

Remember Lydia's reproductive miracle? When the revelation of God's holy sign within her own anatomy hit her heart, she made a bold request of God.

"Lord, would You restore my virginity?"

She didn't mean merely spiritually, but physically. She'd repented of her sins. She knew she'd been forgiven, but she also knew when the spirit of revelation comes, so often follows faith for God's miraculous work. Providentially, our church leadership had at that same time come across the testimony of another minister with similar insight into God's intent for virginity. In a podcast, pastor Kris Vallotton from

Bethel Church in Redding, California, had shared how his daughter-in-law's hymen had grown back after she asked God for restoration, just before her honeymoon with Kris' son. On her wedding night, she phoned Kris crying. Startled by the seemingly untimely call, Kris was at first concerned. Then, through tears, his daughter-in-law began to proclaim, "He did it! God healed me. My hymen grew back!"

This story was all the confirmation my own friend Lydia needed. She believed and called it done in the name of Jesus. A few months later, that routine checkup with her gynecologist revealed a miracle. God did what many physicians deem impossible. He re-created that part of her physical anatomy!

Unveiled Fruit

I'll never forget the first time I shared this "unveiling" truth and personal miracle testimony with a group of our church's young adults. By the end, the girls were in awe, and many of the young men were crying. One teenage boy apologized to his girlfriend for his previous lack of understanding and reverence for the beauty of God's creation in her.

A time of repentance ensued, and many took fresh vows of purity with excitement. No longer did they feel "no sex before marriage" to be a hard command from a mysterious God. Now, they understood the beauty of virginity from a heart level. The men held the women in higher honor, and the women understood that a sign and wonder of Christ's covenant with the church was contained within their bodies.

Fullness of Love

In Christ, the veil is taken away (see 2 Cor. 3:18). What then are the spiritual implications of this torn veil? Christ's shedding of blood made us partakers of a new covenant. That covenant is now based upon faith rather than law. Law is according to our works, but faith works by love (see Gal. 5). Love is about intimacy, the adventure of discovering the depths of another. Before Christ's sacrifice, we were unable to know the Father intimately. Now, though, Jesus has made a way for us not only to be forgiven, not only to become sons and daughters and siblings to Christ, but to boldly come into His Presence and commune as a bride would with her adoring Husband. We are now invited into the endless depths of God's love!

> *So that Christ may dwell in your hearts through faith; and that you, being rooted and grounded in love, may be able to comprehend with all the saints what is the width and length and height and depth, and to know the love of Christ which surpasses knowledge, that you may be filled up to all the fullness of God* **(Ephesians 3:17-19).**

Did you catch the conclusion of verse 19? Paul declared the path to partaking of the fullness of God is *knowing the love of Christ which surpasses knowledge!* In other words, he said the mind is not enough. This love must go deeper. It must become experiential, piercing our very souls and spirits.

God Expects Emotion

To some in the body of Christ, emotion is of grave threat to sound doctrine. They often equate laughing, crying, lifting hands or dancing in worship, for example, with trite, fleeting emotional responses to God.

But the Scripture doesn't say the emotions of a born-again believer are trite. On the contrary, the heart and soul of an unregenerate sinner may be "desperately wicked" (see Jer. 17:9), but when a person becomes born again the situation changes. God doesn't save the spirit and body only. He begins regenerating the soul also. If this were not the case, the human mind itself could not come into sanctification, as the soul generally consists of mind, will, and emotions (or seat of affections).

The most foundational of Scriptures, one quoted by Jesus Himself, states, "Love the Lord your God with all your heart, and with all your *soul*, and with all your strength, and with all your mind" (Luke 10:27). *Heart* and *soul* are right next to *mind* in the list. In other words, love the Lord with every fiber of your created being. Unless you're a robot, that includes the emotions. It's not an option!

Can any marriage thrive without this emotional component? Are there any wives shouting from the rooftops, "My husband loves me so much, he shows no emotion about it!" Of course not. That'd be absurd, supremely dysfunctional. In fact, you'd be hard-pressed to find any couple in a thriving marital communion without engagement of the emotional realm, in addition to mind and body.

> *You have made my heart beat faster, my sister, my bride; you have made my heart beat faster with a single glance of your eyes, with a single strand of your necklace* **(Song of Solomon 4:9).**

God's heart pounds for us! He is emotional about it. That's the Word of God talking, not me! Should we dare deny Him this expression of love? Should we offer anything less in return? It seems to me the more grievous thing to God would be expressing more emotion over natural things than God Himself. If we laugh more at a comedian than we do in His Presence, what gives? If we cry more over a loved one on earth than the Lord of heaven, what gives? If we experience more romance with an earthly partner than our eternal One, what gives?

Contrived expression is one thing, but the idea that we shouldn't show great emotion, or that the Holy Spirit wouldn't elicit it from our created being in adoration to God, is ludicrous. According to Scripture, our greatest emotions should be demonstrated toward God!

> *At that same time Jesus was filled with the joy of the Holy Spirit, and he said, "O Father, Lord of heaven and earth, thank you for hiding these things from those who think themselves wise and clever, and*

for revealing them to the childlike. Yes, Father, it pleased you to do it this way" **(Luke 10:21 NLT).**

Save some cases of psychological or soulish trauma God would desire to heal, emotionless Christianity points to a lack of revelation of God's love. If Jesus commands us to love God with every part of our being, and the apostle John declares, "We love, because He first loved us" (1 John 4:19), it stands to reason that in order to love greater, we need greater understanding of God's love. Remember, Paul states this is not a static, mental ascent to the love Christ once demonstrated on the cross (massive a demonstration as that was), but a fluid, ongoing love flowing from the resurrected One.

To know the love of Christ which surpasses knowledge, that you may be filled up to all the fullness of God **(Ephesians 3:19).**

Now, someone might say, "All of this sounds grandiose. We are not in heaven yet. Our relationship with God can't be all sunshine and rainbows."

It's certainly true that we are not presently living in a physical heaven with the Father Himself. The glories there will certainly surpass the glories here. Yet as we'll explore in the latter parts of this book, many Christians have underestimated the possibilities of the kingdom of God present here. Remember, Paul begins his Ephesians discourse with a prayer that we would acquire greater comprehension of the riches of glorious inheritance offered in Christ Jesus. The context is not merely of a life to come, but the new life we now live!

I pray that the eyes of your heart may be enlightened, so that you will know what is the hope of His calling, what are the riches of the glory of His inheritance in the saints, and what is the surpassing greatness of His power toward us who believe **(Ephesians 1:18-19).**

Now to Him who is able to do far more abundantly beyond all that we ask or think, according to the power that works within us **(Ephesians 3:20).**

That "power toward us" is already here, living within us. It only needs to be accessed through an abiding relationship with the Holy Spirit. One day, we will see Jesus face to face, in the full manifestation of heavenly realms (see 1 Cor. 13:12; 15:25-28). We rightly long for that. We rightly lay up treasure in heaven by sacrificing, stewarding, and keeping an eternal mindset in all we do. Still, we are not there yet. God did not take us into the third heaven the moment we became born again. We are still on earth for a reason. It'd do us well to discover all that is available in God here. Jesus may be our Bridegroom in a physical heaven, but the Scripture declares the Holy Spirit is our fiancé present now on earth (see 2 Cor. 1:22). Heaven ought not be an escape, but a culmination of the romance with God we're cultivating here and now.

My beloved is like a gazelle or a young stag. Behold, he is standing behind our wall, He is looking through the windows, He is peering through the lattice. My beloved responded and said to me, "Arise, my darling, my beautiful one, and come along" **(Song of Solomon 2:9-10).**

Note

1. Ruth Langer, "The Birkat Betulim: A Study of the Jewish Celebration of Bridal Virginity," *Proceedings of the American Academy for Jewish Research*, vol. 61, 1995, 53–94, JSTOR, www.jstor.org/stable/4618851, accessed July 3, 2021.

CHAPTER 8

ARKS OF FRIENDSHIP

Thus far, we've discussed several facets of divine relationship. You may have noticed by now the way in which I've structured them in this book hasn't been arbitrary. Creator, Savior, Lord, Father, Brother, and Bridegroom—this list is progressive in relational proximity.

Now, one might initially think the marital relationship to be ultimate. It can certainly be profoundly intimate. But I do not believe divine marriage to be the absolute closest relation to God's heart. For two people can be legally wed, and yet still drift apart. No, I believe *friendship* to be God's greatest desire for intimacy with His people.

Face to Face

At Mount Sinai, God gave an invitation to the entire nation of Israel to enter direct conversation with Him. Unfortunately,

Israel rejected that invitation. They instead asked Moses to speak to and on behalf of God. What happened? The nation of Israel stopped with a form of legal adoption. God desired their friendship, but they wanted the bare minimum to survive. So, that's what they got—rules and rewards. Moses, however, desired God for God. He gave up all rights of selfish autonomy and instead surrendered his all—heart, mind, soul, and body—to the goal of union with Him.

> *Thus the Lord used to speak to Moses face to face, just as a man speaks to a friend* **(Exodus 33:11).**

God considered a mere man His friend? Yes, and not only that, but Moses was considered such a friend of God that on several occasions God is recorded as even changing His mind after conversation with him!

> *So, the Lord said, "I have pardoned them according to your* [Moses'] *word"* **(Numbers 14:20).**

In Exodus 33, we read God was so angry with the Israelites, He declared He'd wipe them from the face of the earth, only to start over with Moses himself. But after Moses humbly protested—citing God's character and unfailing promises as reasons for not destroying the nation—God answered:

> *The Lord said to Moses, "I will also do this thing of which you have spoken; for you have found favor in My sight and I have known you by name"* **(Exodus 33:17).**

Now, there is considerable theological debate as to whether God actually changed His mind from the divine point of view, or merely from Moses', but suffice to say for our context, friendly negotiation took place. God responded to Moses in a way He clearly did not to others! Lest we be tempted to consider Moses solely unique in this opportunity for friendship, the Bible gives us several examples of men and women who moved His heart in similar ways. Abraham was called God's friend. David was also. Mary and Martha in the gospels were close friends of Jesus. As with Moses, the stories of each of these men and women reveal an intimacy with God so great that He even allowed for friendly negotiation!

So, is this type of relationship possible for us? Is God still looking for and accepting close friends? More than ever!

Arks of a New Covenant

Part of the Mosaic law involved the tabernacle (and later the temple) with its strict ordinances. Although it appears this system was not God's first desire for His people, in His manifold wisdom He crafted a brilliant symbolic message through it. Ironically, the Prophetic Schemer used the very structure and ordinances of the tabernacle (and later temple) built upon legalism to speak to future generations about His desire for friendship!

The tabernacle and temple consisted of three general parts. The innermost place was called the Holy of Holies, where the ark of the covenant dwelled. It is where God Himself would come down to speak to those select few friends He'd chosen to meet with face to face. The New Testament tells us the tabernacle and temple in the Old Testament were prophetic "types." They were symbolic of what was to come. Hebrews explains that these were replicas of a greater, more literal temple in the third heaven, where God the Father dwells (see Heb. 8:5).

However, Paul's letters explain that they were also prophetic imagery for a new type of temple that would one day exist here on the earth.

See, we humans also consist of three parts—spirit, soul, and body (see 1 Thess. 5:23). When Christ shed His blood for the sins of humanity, He fashioned brand-new temples, holy vessels to dwell in. These were not made of stone and mortar. These were made of flesh and blood. That is you and me! We are the temples God always wanted. We are the arks of His new covenant. He isn't looking to fill another building constructed by human hands. He wants to make His own creation His house of glory!

> *Or do you not know that your body is a temple of the Holy Spirit who is in you?* **(1 Corinthians 6:19)**

It's important to note that the Greek word used for *temple* in this passage is more precise than the entire temple structure. *Hieron* is the Greek word meaning the temple at large. Paul, however, uses the word *naos*, which means "the innermost holy place of the Temple where God dwelt." Paul is wanting believers to understand that their bodies are the most intimate dwelling places of the Holy Spirit! Inside our temple, there is no spiritual veil, nothing separating us from communion. So, God's friendship is always within reach. If in Christ, we are now literally the room in which His Presence dwells.

> *Yet the body is not for immorality, but for the Lord, and the Lord is for the body* **(1 Corinthians 6:13).**

So then, the pertinent question isn't necessarily, "Is friendship with God possible?" The pertinent question is, *how do we cultivate friendship with Jesus already in our "room"?*

The Holy Spirit

Up to this point, I've talked much about the Father and the Son, Jesus Christ. But if we're going to talk about the kingdom of God with us, here, now, within human temples upon the earth, we must dive deeper into understanding the Holy Spirit. There's much to say about this Third Person of the Godhead, but for context of friendship with God, it is most vital that we grasp—the Holy Spirit is not an impersonal, mystical force. He's not a distant cousin to Jesus. He is the Lord Himself; He *is* God.

> *Now the Lord is the Spirit* **(2 Corinthians 3:17).**

The Holy Spirit is One with God the Father and the Son, distinct in His Personhood, but Deity nonetheless. In the book of Acts, Luke calls Him the Spirit of Jesus (see Acts 16:7). He is also *the* facilitator of the kingdom of heaven on earth. The kingdom is in the Spirit and manifests through Him. If you've ever prayed, "God, show me Your kingdom," He answers by saying, "I'll show you the Holy Spirit!"

> *For the kingdom of God is...righteousness and peace and joy in the Holy Spirit* **(Romans 14:17).**

Unless Christ appears in bodily form, the Holy Spirit is Jesus in the room—and that "room" entails not only the natural spaces around us, but our very bodies. Therefore, we ought to engage the Holy Spirit by name regularly.

> *The grace of the Lord Jesus Christ, and the love of God, and the fellowship of the Holy Spirit, be with you all* **(2 Corinthians 13:14).**

The Father is in the third heaven (see Matt. 6:9). Christ is seated at His right hand (see Rom. 8:34). But the Holy Spirit is the only God left on earth! I propose that we cannot even know Jesus relationally apart from the Holy Spirit.

> *But when He, the Spirit of truth, comes, He will guide you into all the truth; for He will not speak on His own initiative, but whatever He hears, He will speak; and He will disclose to you what is to come. He will glorify Me, for He will take of Mine and will disclose it to you* **(John 16:13-14).**

No wonder the devil fights the things of the Holy Spirit so hard, even within the church! If he can persuade a believer to shy away from the things of the Spirit, he can effectively deafen their spiritual ears. He can cut off their very source of fellowship and friendship with God.

Parakletos

> *I will ask the Father, and He will give you another Helper, that He may be with you forever; that is the Spirit of truth...you know Him because He abides with you and will be in you* **(John 14:16-17).**

In the original Greek, *Helper* or *Advocate*, as some translations read, is the word *parakletos*. This word's most literal meaning is "one who walks alongside [to help]." The depiction here is that of a best friend!

> *There is a friend who sticks closer than a brother* **(Proverbs 18:24).**

A few years ago, I was ministering to a woman who began manifesting a demonic spirit. I took authority over it and demanded it leave in the name of Jesus. (I'll explain more about demons in subsequent chapters.) This particular demon was contrary, though, even argumentative. It had to leave by the authority of Christ's name, but it wanted to put up a bit of fuss first.

In a moment of sudden inspiration, I remembered that Jesus referred to the Holy Spirit as a helper. Knowing the fuller meaning of this word, I felt like praying to His Greek name. I said, "Parakletos, my Friend, I ask You to help enforce this situation. Make this demon submit." Suddenly, the demon went from a somewhat calm and mocking demeanor to shrieking as if in terror. "NOOOOO!" it exclaimed, before ultimately leaving the person.

Now, speaking Greek is not a formula for deliverance. The point I'm trying to make here is that even demon spirits understand the power and authority of the Holy Spirit when a believer honors and cultivates a relationship with Him. Thank God I had! My friendship with the Holy Spirit was not always so secure though. God had to teach me progressively through the years. He did this through the Scripture, but also personal encounters. One such personal interaction with the Spirit truly changed the way I viewed my relationship with God forever. I pray it does the same for you!

I Hurt God's Heart

"You've offended the Lord!" his voice sternly said.

I could scarcely think of hearing something more egregious from a prophet. Besides receiving a rare judgment of death, as with, for example, Ananias and Sapphira (Acts 5), personally offending God has got to make a top list of things you'd never want to do. Thankfully, that wasn't the end of the prophecy. In fact, the clarifying conclusion became what I still consider the greatest prophecy I've ever received.

At the time of this story, I'd been pastoring for several years at our local church. We had consistently experienced glorious outpourings of the Presence of God, salvations, healings, and numerous miracles. Yet, as any pastor knows, seasons in ministry aren't without trials.

For reasons I can't fully remember, this particular week had been unusually stressful. As had become my custom, I decided to spend some time one evening praying in the front section of our church. Although I knew God was present, to be honest, at that moment He felt to me a thousand miles away. Several issues I'd been contending for in prayer had yet to see a breakthrough. I was tired, discouraged, and feeling desperately lonely.

As I paced the floor, Bible stories of men and women having fantastic encounters with God flooded my mind. This time, however, it wasn't a recall that inspired faith. On the contrary, I was splashing in a pool of self-pity, considering I'd become an exception to God's nearness. In frustration, I spoke too candidly to God.

"Where are You!?" I shouted. "We've known each other for years, but I'm starting to wonder how close we actually are. You say I'm Your friend, but am I really?"

A kind of temporary amnesia was setting in, and in that moment, my history with Jesus seemed lost in my memory. I continued, "I know You say I'm Your friend theologically, but can we get real here? I'm not so sure I even know You. I'm not sure You've ever called me friend!"

A quiet angst filled the air for a few moments, as I continued pacing back and forth on the carpet. Then, unexpectedly, a text message notification came through on my phone.

Who would be texting me after midnight? I thought.

I reached up to the pulpit where my phone lay, grabbed it and looked at the screen. My friend, Todd Dawkins, had sent a message. I knew from a previous conversation that he was in another part of the state, driving in his car.

His message said, "What are you doing right now?"

My thumbs tapped each letter with more irritated force than usual. "I'm at the church, praying."

He said, "Call me!"

Reluctantly, I acquiesced. Todd immediately picked up. He asked once more, "What are you doing?" Trying to conceal exasperation for his redundancy, I replied, "I'm just praying." He then sternly said those words I'll never forget.

"You've offended the Lord!"

Having lost my usual mouth filter to the midnight hour, I mused, "Oh great! When it rains it pours!" Then Todd more fully explained, "No, you've offended the Lord. How dare you say that you are not His friend!?"

My mouth dropped open. The accuracy of this prophetic word was impossible. The timing was too coincidental. Todd continued, "A few minutes ago, I saw a mind's eye vision of you while driving. The Holy Spirit said, 'Tell Josh, "I'm hurt that He doubts our friendship."'"

Todd then went on to prophesy that God considered me one of His trusted friends—that I had cultivated years of history with Him, and because of my repeated obedience to His voice, He considered me close to His heart. He added that Jesus also planned to draw me into greater depths of intimacy in my latter years, and it would fulfill deep longings within me.

I wept. Doubts in my relationship with Jesus had literally hurt Him. He considered our friendship such a precious thing, He had a prophet answer my complaints less than five minutes after I had offered them in private! Through tears of joy, I apologized to God for doubting His nearness. My heart filled with gratitude, and I worshiped.

I've received many prophetic words in my life. Some about my ministry, about doors God wanted to open to influence regions or people groups. Others were about personal things concerning family or friends. Some words have been so impossibly accurate, the hair on my arms has stood up. Still, I consider the word from Todd that night the greatest prophecy I've ever received. God personally called me friend, in real time. To be declared friends with the King! What could be greater?

> *If there is a prophet among you, I, the Lord, shall make Myself known to him in a vision. I shall speak with him in a dream. Not so, with My servant Moses, he is faithful in all My household; with him I speak mouth to mouth, even openly, and not in dark sayings, and he beholds the form of the Lord* **(Numbers 12:6-8).**

The Scripture, from Genesis to maps, is laden with visions, dreams, and symbolic prophecy. In the New Testament, we read these forms of communication are part and parcel to the outpouring of the Holy Spirit upon all flesh (see Acts 2:17-18). Even so, God declared in the book of Numbers that there is a place where He will go beyond symbolism into candid communion. In the days of Israel, that place was reserved for Moses. Through Jesus, God now beckons all who are willing to come and dine directly with Him (see John 21:12).

I'm not saying friends can't have dreams or visions. I'm simply citing a Scripture that indicates the faithful are given a privileged seat at His table. There we encounter Him not as a symbolic shadow, but as an unveiled Friend.

Closer Than We Think

Indeed, He is not far from each one of us **(Acts 17:27 YLT).**

God's heart must be grieved that many believers live as though their relationship with Him begins after they die. To them, Christianity is a type of blind faith, hoping to one day escape the isolated misery of this earthly existence. But God doesn't want us living this way! While the glories of heaven to come will certainly surpass those of this life, Christ stated the ultimate purpose for His sacrifice wasn't to one day take us to the "sweet by and by." No, Christ said the first definition of eternal life was to *know* Him!

> *This is eternal life, that they may know You, the only true God, and Jesus Christ whom You have sent* **(John 17:3).**

Know here is the Greek word *ginosko*. It is a word with many layers of meaning. In the Old Testament Greek Septuagint, *ginosko* is often used in place of the original Hebrew word *yada*. *Yada*, like *ginosko*, is also a multi-dimensional word. One such dimension and use of it is when speaking of Moses' face-to-face encounter with God! However, *yada* can also be found all the way back in the garden of Eden account. The context there? Sexual intimacy between Adam and Eve.

> *And Adam knew* [yada] *Eve his wife; and she conceived* **(Genesis 4:1 KJV).**

Now, obviously, I'm not suggesting something perverse in our relationship with God. The reference is of merit though, as even amidst sexual union there are the deepest layers of spiritual and soulish exchange. Christ is saying He, too, desires this intimacy. He longs to spiritually fellowship as a husband and wife who remain close friends.

Keeping Trust

One of the greatest privileges of friendship with God is His trust. Jesus loves everyone, but He can't trust everyone!

> *But Jesus, on His part, was not entrusting Himself to them, for He knew all men* **(John 2:24).**

One Sunday evening, a young man in his early 20s approached me at the altar. He shared that he'd been called to full-time ministry but feared becoming prideful. He'd recently tasted the temptation of being looked up to, including by many young Christian women. He was fearful of letting it go to his head.

"I've watched you for a while, and you seem to have (so far) avoided these kinds of things," he said. "How have you remained humble?"

I responded, "First, the fact you are acknowledging that temptation so openly shows me that you actually have a humble heart. Temptation comes to us all, but humility asks for help! Great job.

"As for how I've stayed humble overall," I continued, "I'm a man just like you. I've made mistakes and needed Jesus' forgiveness, but there are two chief motivations I've learned to always keep in my heart. First, I know that if Jesus hadn't saved me, I'd be lost. If He hadn't called me, I'd have no ministry. If His Presence doesn't manifest in my life, I have no power and bear no real fruit. Without Him, I'm just a talking head. I'm truly *nothing*. The same goes for you."

Taking a step back, he responded, "Wow, that's heavy. It's true though, I guess."

"Yes, it is," I said. "Secondly, there is truly no greater desire in my heart than to have His trust. I mean, that of a close friend. Imagine the King of the universe choosing to walk with you, sharing secrets He can't entrust to everyone. Brother, I can't think of a greater reward for humility than that. Humility and trust, then, must remain our deepest desires. If we can simply keep these two heart postures, we'll not fail."

The young man responded well to my advice. On my way home, I thought about that second motivation again for my own life and began to cry. I thought about moments He'd shared secrets with me. At times, He'd even entrusted me with prophetic insights into people's most vulnerable life situations, including that of a few well-known individuals in secular industries. No doubt, He did this hoping I'd steward it well. He hoped I'd not use inside information to manipulate for personal gain. He hoped I'd protect their hearts and His.

I also thought about the times I'd fallen short of His trust—times I'd been less than faithful and yet He picked me back up. When I fell to my knees in confession of my weakness, my Friend still came running. One such encounter reminds me of His kindness perhaps above all others.

Merciful Friend

I had sinned. I knew better. I had felt the conviction of the Spirit, yet I chose to go forward anyway. Feelings of shame and embarrassment flooded my mind and soul. The last thing my flesh wanted to do was run into God's holy Presence. Yet, I thought, "What good is all that I've learned, all that I've taught and imparted to others if I, too, do not live it?"

I couldn't hide from God as Adam and Eve did. I knew I needed to run once more into His arms. So, I got dressed and took the short walk through the humid summer air from my house to our church. No one was there and I knew I'd be all alone in the dark with God. I entered the building and put on a soft worship instrumental to help calm my anxieties. For the first few minutes, I paced quietly, posturing my heart humbly before the Lord. Then, I began to weep. For nearly half an hour, I poured out tears of heartfelt repentance.

I then cried out, "Jesus, please forgive me. I know You will, but I'm telling You from the depth of my heart that I want to live holy to please You. I want to be faithful, without hypocrisy. Please give me grace to better walk this out."

Heavy weeping turned to gentle tears as I pivoted to worship Him. Although I knew I'd sinned, I equally knew His Word said He was "faithful and just to forgive" that which I confessed. Now, it was appropriate to let the blood of Jesus cleanse my conscience—to believe Christ had blotted the incident completely from my record.

I remained in that space for another half hour, worshiping and pouring my love out to my Lord. Just then, I heard the front door of the sanctuary open. Only a few people had keys to the church, so I wasn't alarmed. It was still very dark though, and I couldn't make out who the visitor was. I assumed they'd come to retrieve something, or perhaps quietly pray. So, I did not outwardly acknowledge them.

A few seconds later, though, I heard a tremendous crash. When I turned around to observe the source, I noticed the person who'd entered was one of my church leaders, and she was now lying on the floor. Several chairs were out of place, as she had apparently knocked them over on her way down.

Her voice rang out in the dark, "What are you doing in here!?" she asked. "I just came in to grab something, and I can't stand up! God's Presence is so heavy."

I was stunned. As I remained on my knees in prayer, I hadn't noticed the manifest Presence of God flooding the sanctuary. Then it hit me. The Holy Spirit had chosen to draw near, but not in a moment of triumph. I hadn't demonstrated some great measure of faith, nor delivered a fiery sermon to His liking. No, He literally drew near while I was openly confessing my sin! Although He is the Holy King, He is also a merciful Father, an understanding Brother and faithful Friend. I wept tears of joy at the thought of this act of divine kindness. In fact, tears flow even now as I recount it for you.

> *When he* [a righteous man] *falls, he will not be hurled headlong, because the Lord is the One who holds his hand* **(Psalm 37:24).**

Intimacy with God is the great equalizer. Money can't buy His friendship. Social media follows won't earn His favor. Self-promotion can't clothe us in His Presence. We may fool people, but we can't fool God. We must remain true to our divine friendship in secret, so that heaven may proudly vouch for us in public. When our private walks with Jesus are healthy and thriving, heaven is accessible to us—because all of heaven is *in* Christ!

We are invited to be best friends with the Great King. In that fellowship, we shouldn't just seek His love, we should seek His trust. Friendship with God is a highly privileged position, after all! He offers us His heart. Will you accept that invitation as Moses once did? Will you value and honor His Presence above all others?

> *The secret [of the wise counsel] of the Lord is for those who fear Him, and He will let them know His covenant and reveal to them [through His word] its [deep, inner] meaning* **(Psalm 25:14 AMP).**

Keys to Divine Friendship

Below is a bullet point list of keys for drawing the Presence of God near. Remember, friendship is not a formula, but these biblical principles will help you to better understand God's ways. They've helped me to maintain and grow a deep and thriving friendship with Jesus. I've included several corresponding Scriptures for each, and strongly encourage you to take a moment to study them.

Remember, Jesus *wants* to be your friend. He's invited you into His innermost chambers! These are keys to His door:

- Faith (Heb. 11:6; Eph. 3:17)
- Humility (James 4:6; Isa. 57:15; Prov. 22:4)
- Hunger (Exod. 33:11; Matt. 15:22-28)
- Worship (Rom. 12:1; 1 Chron. 16:23-31; 2 Chron. 5:13-14)
- Prayer (James 4:8; Ps. 145:18; Luke 5:16)
- Obedience (John 14:21; John 15:14; Acts 5:32)

SECTION 3

MANIFESTATION

CHAPTER 9

TALKING WITH GOD

Language is in everything. Beyond literal words and syllables, the sun, stars, seasons, and sounds all communicate messages. Wind howls. Trees whisper. Animals sing. Language is even revealed in the advent of life and death. All of creation communicates a voice, because it came from *the* Voice—the Word of God.

Eden unveils the character of Christ's creative Word. We see therein His unfathomable power and majesty. Yet we also observe His love, artistry, and even the humorous side. Some of God's animals look and act very funny! When I began to recognize this broader Voice, it opened entirely new dimensions of what we often refer to as *the prophetic*. Now, the word *dimensions* in our culture sometimes carries a new-age connotation, but this is not how I mean it. I'm referring to the fact the Scripture says all of creation is from, through, and for Christ. So, He's not merely limited to spoken words. No,

Jesus has placed language in all parts of creation, because He literally embodies it; language is in His very name.

> *In the beginning was the Word* [Jesus] **(John 1:1).**

Paul reiterates the ever-living echo of His voice in creation in saying:

> *For since the creation of the world His invisible attributes, His eternal power and divine nature, have been clearly seen, being understood through what has been made, so that they are without excuse* **(Romans 1:20).**

His Voice in Scripture

Few Christians dispute the value of the written Word of God. Many, however, question its measure of authority. There has been great effort especially in recent times to discredit and "deconstruct" the Bible. Liberal scholars and readers alike have often sought to deem vast portions of the texts as mere metaphor, good only for psychological and sociological study. They do not believe its contents ought to be taken as divine utterance.

The trouble with that reasoning is the Scripture declares itself to be much more than terrestrial in origin and authority.

> *All Scripture is inspired by God and profitable for teaching, for reproof, for correction, for training in*

righteousness; so that the man of God may be adequate, equipped for every good work **(2 Timothy 3:16-17).**

Jesus trusted the Scripture's divine authority so much, He declared it "cannot be broken" (see John 10:35). He used the texts to teach, admonish, and argue for God's intended instructions since ancient times. He even used "it is written" to rebuke the devil to his face!

Without the Scripture, all history of God's dealings with humanity would be left to mere hearsay. We'd have no record of His love, His justice, or His righteous acts among mankind through the ages. Consequently, our sense of morality would be without surety. Moreover, without the writings of the law and the prophets, there'd be no foretelling of Christ nor reason given for His coming. The gospel itself would die the death of a thousand subjective opinions. In short, without the Scripture, we'd be lost, having no anchor for our souls.

It is no wonder then the Holy Spirit so distinctly instructed me in my early days of following Christ, "Learn My written Word first." For the Scripture not only reveals God's consistent nature and ways but illuminates the very paths of life itself.

Your word is a lamp to my feet, and a light to my path **(Psalm 119:105).**

Before Christ changed my heart, I could barely understand a single parable in the gospels. Now, I can scarcely read a passage of the Bible without some word or sentence being shot from the page as an arrow into my heart. God desires the same for you! His voice *is* ever present in His written Word. There is no book like it in the world. For those reading with humility and a teachable ear bent toward the Spirit of God, the Scripture will be living and active. Through the Bible, God can open the libraries of ancient history, and yet speak prophetic wisdom to a real-time scenario in the 21st century.

> *For the word of God is living and active and sharper than any two-edged sword and piercing as far as the division of soul and spirit, of both joints and marrow, and able to judge the thoughts and intentions of the heart* **(Hebrews 4:12).**

Now, while the Scripture is a foundation from which God speaks, it is not intended to be the whole house. This is where some in the body of Christ may differ in theological belief, but in rigidly refusing to accept any other instrument through which God speaks, they risk the very error of the Pharisees and Sadducees, who missed their own Messiah. Jesus said:

> *You search the Scriptures because you think that in them you have eternal life; it is these that testify about Me* **(John 5:39).**

The religious leaders of Jesus' day had a difficult time with the living, breathing personification of God. Their intellectual pride and often one-dimensional obsession with the written Scripture led them to miss the Messiah's coming. They believed their traditions and doctrinal interpretations reigned supreme. When Jesus came on the scene, however, He demonstrated what God really meant in those Scriptures by confirming His interpretations with great supernatural power.

> *But the testimony which I have is greater than the testimony of John; for the works which the Father has given Me to accomplish—the very works that I do—testify about Me, that the Father has sent Me* **(John 5:36).**

The Father backed Christ's teachings and the religious leaders hated Him for it. They hated that the Holy Spirit sometimes did works outside of their box of understanding. Of course, the things Jesus did weren't actually in contradiction to the Scripture, merely many of the religious leaders' presuppositions. Jesus confronted their error in not dismissing Scripture, but saying He was the One spoken of within them; Christ the Person was the ultimate goal!

Thus, the Bible is not a spiritual ceiling, but a floor. Its precepts keep us securely on the right path. It ought to never be contradicted, but it ought not be the totality of our experience with its Author. No, the purpose of the Word is to lead us to the Person of the Word! Without encountering and interacting with its Author, our relationship with Scripture becomes merely lifeless, historical information. In fact, the Scripture itself says that without the Holy Spirit's Presence, "the letter kills" (2 Cor. 3:6)!

So then, the Spirit and the Word are not to be pitted against one another, as if they belong to two camps of Christian belief. They are to be married and remain that way! They are to work together, confirming and affirming our relationship in Spirit and in truth.

> *God is spirit, and those who worship Him must worship in spirit and in truth* **(John 4:24).**

His Voice in Prayer

Entire libraries of material could be written about prayer. Indeed, they have been. I've learned much from such books, written by incredible men and women of God. For the purpose of this writing, however, I am going to focus on what I believe are some of the more overlooked, yet key principles for prayer. These were truths that took me years to realize, and I hope to circumvent years of that journey for you.

While many aspects of my young walk with God seemed to consistently grow, my prayer life had stagnated. To be honest, even after encountering the power of the Spirit in my 20s, my prayer life hadn't graduated beyond a first-grade level. I was ashamed to admit I didn't really know how to be alone with God for more than a few minutes without spacing out or getting bored.

Like a good Christian boy, though, I soldiered on. I studied different types of prayer: Jesus' model, petitions, intercessions, prayers of faith, and more. To be sure, these are all valid, but even after practicing them, I still couldn't find my sweet spot with the Lord. At one point, I thought pounding on the ground and literally screaming at the top of my lungs would get God's attention. It didn't seem to. I was frustrated.

Finally, after exhausting all known avenues of study, I was down to every young man's last resort for advice—dad.

Truthfully, I had tremendous respect for my father, Mike Adkins. He traveled the world ministering the gospel and was known for his consistent integrity and obedience to God. I knew it was a distinct privilege growing up beneath his example. I hadn't asked his advice on prayer though, because for most of my childhood he'd kept his *secret place* rather secret. I wasn't sure what his prayer life looked like practically, yet I knew he heard from God.

As a young boy riding in the passenger seat to his meetings, I can recall one time asking, "Dad, what are you going to speak on tonight?"

He replied, "I don't know. God hasn't told me yet."

"Hasn't told you yet!?" I scoffed. How could he be so calm? We were pulling up to the doors of the church. There were hundreds of people waiting inside, and my father, their guest speaker, expected to give an insightful monologue for nearly an hour, had no idea what he was going to say? How could he not be sweating through his shirt or suffering from stress-induced diarrhea? Yet there he was, calm as a cucumber, ready to shake hands and speak with the people.

This scenario played out more times than I can recount. When my dad finally would step up to the platform, he never seemed devoid of inspired speech. He would act on inward promptings from the Holy Spirit, and miracles would often break out immediately, right before our eyes. As a young man, I felt like royalty being the son of a man who could so easily hear God's voice. But when I became a man myself, I realized I could no longer merely play in my natural father's palace. God wanted me to learn His ways for myself. This had all brought me to an impasse.

Finally, I humbled myself and asked, "Dad, I'm at my wits' end. I've been begging God to talk to me. Sometimes I pray for hours, but I still can't hear the Holy Spirit like you do."

He responded, "Well, son. You don't have to beg God to speak. Have you tried just listening?"

Offended by such a simple suggestion, I retorted, "What do you mean, 'just listening'? I'm talking about really hearing God's voice here!"

He grinned, "So am I. If you've begged and pleaded and it's not gotten you anywhere, why not try relaxing instead? God knows your heart. If you listen with peace, He'll speak to you."

Though his seemingly cavalier advice flustered me in the moment, I knew he was right. I had been striving. The trouble was, I didn't know how not to! The next day I woke up and decided to pray for no more than a few minutes. Then, I exhaled and went about my day. Certain this would only pull me further from God, I was already rehearsing telling my father his advice was of no help. That afternoon, though, as I walked through the living room, I suddenly heard that same voice I had in the very beginning of my journey! The Holy Spirit whispered, "Josh, throw away all of your music CDs.

You listen to them nonstop in your car, and that's one of the places I want to talk to you."

I was stunned. I'd been straining for months to hear God and received nothing. Now, if I were making things up, I'd surely not have come up with that idea! I had amassed hundreds of dollars in CDs. I listened to them around the clock. One might think I'd be reluctant then to toss out objects of that much value, but the truth was, the moment I believed I'd heard Jesus, I couldn't get to the dumpster fast enough. I also knew why He had instructed me to do this. It was one of the chief distractions keeping me from hearing His voice.

> *Therefore if you have been raised up with Christ, keep seeking the things above, where Christ is, seated at the right hand of God. Set your mind on the things above, not on the things that are on earth* **(Colossians 3:1-2).**

Guess what happened? I began to hear God's voice daily on my drives! Then I understood: I didn't have to strive. The Lord was always near. My mind had just been so full of other noise, I couldn't hear Him. I was looking for a booming voice to cut through my cluttered life, when God desired to speak in a still, small one.

> *After the wind there was an earthquake, but the Lord was not in the earthquake. And after the earthquake there was a fire, but the Lord was not in the fire. And after the fire there was the sound of a gentle whisper* **(1 Kings 19:11-12 NLT).**

I heard someone once say the reason they believed God rarely yells is because He refuses to compete with any other voice. He is too worthy of our first love and attention. This is surely true! Since that day, I've prayed with this revelation intact. I meet with God in my car, in the shower, in parks, or on walking paths. Sometimes I talk for a few minutes. Most of the time, though, I relax and listen with peace. Prayer is now more conversation and less monologue.

Still, God wanted to take me deeper than one lesson.

Silence Is Golden

A few years later, I felt prompted by the Holy Spirit to attend a prayer meeting about six miles away from my hometown. When I walked in the door, I was greeted by the owner of the house, Rita Carlton. She was a gentle, godly woman, known and respected by many in our area for her robust prayer life. After some brief introductions, I walked into the living room to discover I was one of only two people under the age of 50 there! In fact, most of the people who attended her meetings were women *above* that age.

I silently asked, "God, what am I doing here with a bunch of old women?"

I heard no words, but I did have an inward peace. I felt as if I'd just come home, despite never having set foot in this place. I've learned over the years that this drawing of my spirit to calm is another way God speaks. The Spirit leads us into peace. Paul calls it "bearing witness."

> *For all who are being led by the Spirit of God, these are sons of God. ...The Spirit Himself testifies with our spirit* **(Romans 8:14,16).**

Whenever I've followed that inward witness, I've usually found godly fruit. In the case of this prayer meeting, it didn't make sense to my natural mind, but I knew God had me there for a reason.

Now, this meeting was unlike many church meetings I'd been to before. There was no worship music. Bibles were strewn across coffee tables or sitting open next to the women, but instead of teaching planned lessons from the Scripture, they would only occasionally read a passage that seemed highlighted to them in an inspired moment. The majority of the time they spent doing something that up to that point in my life, I'd found very difficult:

They sat in silence.

I don't mean just a few seconds or minutes of silence. I mean the room was so still you could hear a pin drop for sometimes an hour! I don't know if it was the fact I was so unfamiliar, or that I was one of the few in the room housing high levels of testosterone, but I could barely endure this level of stillness. In fact, the first week was like a form of torture! My mind wandered. My chair creaked as I constantly shifted to different positions. It was a fight. Reluctantly though, I endured.

One of those first nights attending, after what seemed like half an hour, my thoughts finally began to settle. That's when a picture suddenly flashed across my mind. It seemed the faintest impression, one I'd likely have dismissed a thousand times before. Due to the silence, though, I was able to grab hold of it. I pictured a man riding a horse, whipping it harder than a man should. There was strain on his face and sweat upon his brow. (The horse didn't seem happy either.) Figuring I had nothing to lose, I gently broke the room's silence, "I think I may have seen something from the Lord?" Some of the women only slightly lifted their eyes, while others remained completely still.

"Uhh," I nervously stammered. "I saw this horse, with a man furiously riding upon it...." I hadn't finished my description when suddenly one woman began to laugh out loud. Then another. I was so embarrassed. I said, "Hey, please don't laugh at me. I'm doing my best here."

The woman laughing loudest then said, "No, no, son. I'm not laughing at you. I'm laughing because I was seeing a horse too! Very similar to what you described." Another woman then broke in, "Me too! I saw a horse with a rider."

When we compared further mental notes, the message seemed clear. God was showing us that He was speaking about striving. Someone, perhaps multiple people in the room, had been working hard for God, rather than trusting His Spirit to lead them in rest. The "rider," as it were, needed to learn to relax and stop beating his horse.

Perhaps you think this story is mere mystical imagination, but this was truly another turning point for me with prayer.

Week after week, month after month, I returned to this meeting. We often sat in similar silence. In doing so, we heard many prophetic words from God. When we tested them, many times we'd discover immediate confirmation of prayers or situations in our lives. Later, I began to understand this practice of stillness as a theological truth.

True Love Waits

> *Love is patient* **(1 Corinthians 13:4).**

It's love's very first attribute. Patience waits. It trusts. Patient people listen with loving intent to hear and understand. "I waited patiently for the Lord; he turned to me and heard my cry" (Ps. 40:1 NIV).

While there are volumes of insights about prayer, some perhaps still beyond my grasp, one thing particularly that changed my life was discovering it's more beneficial to hear God than for God to hear me! Therefore in prayer, we should often focus more on listening than talking.

> *Guard your steps as you go to the house of God and draw near to listen rather than to offer the sacrifice of fools; for they do not know they are doing evil. Do not be hasty in word or impulsive in thought to bring up a matter in the presence of God* **(Ecclesiastes 5:1-2).**

This is not to say we're bound to legalistic silence in prayer. Obviously, other Scriptures affirm talking freely to God. Nevertheless, it is more beneficial to hear than to speak! When I made this shift, I began hearing the Holy Spirit even more. If not in the silent moments, He'd suddenly break into my mundane thoughts throughout the day. His voice seemed louder, and when I tested His instructions, they bore much fruit!

See, some Christian cultures train people to pray long, repetitious prayers. Others scream in tongues for hours. Well, sometimes God hears long prayers, and tongues is a wonderful gift! I personally pray in tongues every day for reasons I do not have time and space to expound upon in this book. Yet, we can't forget what Paul also said in Corinthians:

> *If I speak with the tongues of men and of angels, but do not have love, I have become a noisy gong or a clanging cymbal* **(1 Corinthians 13:1).**

Jesus also instructed:

> *And when you are praying, do not use meaningless repetition as the Gentiles do, for they suppose that they will be heard for their many words* **(Matthew 6:7).**

I discovered that it's actually possible to scream at God for hours and hear very little back. This is not to say loud prayers aren't at times appropriate. The Bible says Jesus at times offered loud cries and petitions to God (see Heb. 5:7). But if we look at the totality of His life and ministry, we don't see straining and screaming. We see the Messiah living and operating from peace. He seemed to constantly converse with the Father in an effortless manner. Every word He then spoke became prophetic.

> *For I did not speak on My own initiative* **(John 12:49).**

This is prayer *with* God. It is two-way conversation, birthed and sustained from a love relationship. When you're in close proximity to someone, a whisper carries just as much authority as a shout, and it's often more appropriate. Again, there are moments when volume in prayer may be fitting, but you don't have to scream at God to get His attention. Become friends with the King, and you'll find His ear more than bent toward you (see John 15:7).

Not Without Faith

While silence is a powerful practice, I've also seen people sit in prayer rooms for hours a day and still have no power over their own issues, let alone that of others. It's because their prayers aren't combined with faith. Intimacy is two ways, and it produces confidence. That confidence (faith) opens our ears to hear, which results in power. If we as prayer people have little power, it's likely because we have little faith. In that, we may be merely talking at God, rather than *with* Him. Conversely, when we believe He is near—when we draw near with faith and peace to listen—we sow seeds to the Spirit that will reap a greater hearing harvest. God's thoughts can then flow freely from His heaven to our earth, the mind of Christ to the spirit of our mind (see Eph. 4:23).

> *The spirit of man is the lamp of the Lord* **(Proverbs 20:27).**

Now, the Bible has much more to say about prayer. I will expound on a few more types and principles in a moment. Perhaps like me, though, God needs to strip away some of your acquired traditions. Perhaps He needs to remove some measure of religious striving, and instead replace it with a deep revelation of prayer's simplest definition—a conversation between friends.

God Enjoys Our Company

Before my prayer life could fully blossom, God had to teach me at least one more foundational truth about intimacy. Even after learning these lessons, prayer still hadn't become a passion. I struggled to meet regularly with God in the *secret place*. My mind knew I should, but my heart rarely felt the pull to set aside time.

I'd been honestly talking with the Lord about this for a while, when one day, while driving in my car, the Holy Spirit broke in. He said, "Josh, you think of time alone with Me like a vending machine. Put a quarter in and get a quarter's worth of spiritual life out. It's still *a work* (a religious task) for you. Do you not understand, son? I enjoy *your* company."

Wait, God wants to spend time with *me?* He delights in my company, rather than just ordering me to delight in His? Illumination again flooded my heart. I realized once more that Jesus wanted me more than I could want Him. His love was to be my fuel, and it would turn my "quiet time" from mere duty of discipline to a life-filled, relational adventure!

With this heart shift, I began sensing the Lord pulling me into His Presence more often throughout the day. I no longer felt I *had* to get alone with Him. I *wanted* to get alone with Him. Speaking and listening to God while in the car or amidst everyday life was good. I had learned we should invite Him into everything! But now, I more often wanted to give Him my full attention in secret. If I went more than a day or two without this time in the secret place, I'd begin feeling empty. Then, I'd hear that gentle whisper again, "Come away with Me, beloved." I knew there was nothing wrong with an occasional external entertainment with family or friends, but when I'd feel He tugged, my heart would long for His company more than all others.

See, God isn't beckoning us because He requires a time clock to be punched. No, He waits for the sake of fellowship! The Bible even declares He jealously burns to be with us (see James 4:6). The Lord needed me to understand that even my prayer life must stem from the foundations of His love:

> *We love, because He first loved us* **(1 John 4:19).**
>
> *Faith working through love* **(Galatians 5:6).**

Prayer became desirable the moment I truly believed God's promise to draw near. It became intimate when I discovered

He actually enjoyed my company. This is, after all, a God already near to us. He's in us. He's adopted us as royal sons and daughters. He wants to speak to us, and He's made it easy to hear, if only we'll draw near to listen.

> *Draw near to God and He will draw near to you* **(James 4:8).**

His Voice in Dreams

As a teenager in the west, I often heard about "pizza dreams." I was told that food caused strange visions in the night. Likewise, dwelling upon a particular situation, fear, or even a specific person during the day could result in related dreams. For this reason, I placed the entirety of my dream life in a category of dismissal, something unimportant and unworthy of any spiritual consideration.

This is regretful, because while it is certainly true that some dreams seem stimulated by natural causes, the Bible is chock-full of instances of God speaking through them. In fact, both the Old and New Testaments have far more to say about dream life than I've discovered most Christians realize.

A few years ago, I met a woman named Shannon Hess. She had been Roman Catholic for much of her life, until an encounter with the Holy Spirit at one of our church's regional conferences. There she was born again. A few weeks later, she received the baptism in the Holy Spirit.

Shannon grew faster than most in the Lord. Her heart was full of integrity and character. She and her husband Jim were both humble and teachable. Consequently, God accelerated them in knowledge, wisdom, and supernatural gifting. They quickly became powerful leaders in our church community.

One gift given to Shannon was prophetic dreaming. She had dreamed for years before and even kept journals, but often had no understanding of what her dreams meant. However, when Shannon received the baptism in the Holy Spirit, this sovereign gift fell into its rightful place. Christ was now at the helm, and a prolific grace for interpreting dreams came upon Shannon to remain. She would often know details about things in each of our lives at the church, not to mention others in our region. We soon learned God wanted to instruct our entire church body at times through not just her dreams, but the dreams of others also.

Another young woman named Alyssa Galloway emerged as a powerful dreamer and interpreter. She too would sometimes receive messages that were of merit to our entire church community. This type of prophetic guidance was at first a point of caution for several of our leaders, including me. I'd believed for most of my life that dreams were merely a supplemental confirmation of the voice of God, nothing more. There were too many "spooky-spiritual" dreamers out there, I reasoned. Decisions ought to be based upon something more concrete. Right?

While there is certainly merit to testing prophetic utterances (see 1 Cor. 14:29), I couldn't deny the accuracy and wisdom we were gleaning from Shannon's and Alyssa's dreams in particular. That's when I discovered the Bible had more to say about directional dreaming—and in some ways, it disagreed with my presuppositions. (If you hadn't noticed yet, God likes to sometimes upend our theology.)

A few examples of instructional dreams in the New Testament include the angel of the Lord visiting Joseph, directing him to take Jesus to Egypt to avoid the genocide Herod was about to inflict upon the children of Israel (see Matt. 1:20). Another is the dream the apostle Paul received instructing him to go preach in Macedonia (see Acts 16:9-10). Of course, most are familiar with the dreams God gave to a pagan Egyptian pharaoh (see Gen. 41). Through these dreams, the Lord revealed His instructions that in the end saved Egypt and many surrounding nations.

With the example of Pharaoh's dreams, it's important to note that God used Joseph to not only interpret the symbolism, but to bring glory to the God of Israel in doing so. See, Pharaoh wasn't a prophet because he had dreams. Joseph was the prophet because of his gift to interpret them. I'm not suggesting all who interpret dreams are prophets, but that interpreting dreams, rather than merely receiving them, is the greater gift.

On the other hand, for Christians, we do not always need to have an external interpreter of dreams. In the new covenant, all believers have access to the Holy Spirit. So, all ought to pray to interpret their own dream life. God may use other believers from time to time, but just as it is with tongues, He wants to develop every Christian's personal language for understanding messages from Him (see 1 Cor. 14:13). Therefore, we ought to ask Him first for help interpreting, before running to other people, manuals, or search engines. Again, God may use those tools from time to time, but our first interpreter is the Holy Spirit Himself!

My friend Shannon Hess has written an insightful book along these lines called *Dreaming with a Healthy Heart*. It is chock-full of supernatural wisdom and real-life examples of dreams and processes of healthy interpretation. I highly recommend it!

The Weather Man

After the Lord began updating my understanding of prophetic dreaming, I felt led to ask Shannon and a few others whom I knew to be especially gifted in this area to lay hands upon me and pray. Although I was their pastor, I wanted to humble myself and show honor for the greater gift God had given them in this area. I've learned over the years God honors this type of humility, and there is reward in acting upon it!

> *He who receives a prophet in the name of a prophet shall receive a prophet's reward* **(Matthew 10:41).**

To my delight, after receiving this prayer my dream life exploded! I went from prophetically dreaming once every few months to several times a week. For me personally, the dreams were often quite literal, whereas before they seemed vague and/or laden with difficult symbolism. One such dream I had from the Lord literally saved an outreach event our church was conducting to feed, clothe, and bless the needy.

Each year, Loft Church hosts an annual event called "Christmas on the Streets." At this event, we give away thousands of dollars of new or slightly used toys to those struggling to provide their children with gifts for Christmas. We are also privileged to donate coats, shoes, toiletries, and food with no strings attached. There's even a "big ticket" item raffle where we give away prizes like flat screen TVs, bicycles, and more. It's our favorite event each year.

But many don't know, the very first time we hosted this event, it almost didn't happen. If not for the Lord, we may have had such a bad experience we'd have foregone any other attempts.

We called it "Christmas on the Streets" because our initial plan was to rent a giant tent for a city block. As you can imagine, the logistics for this event needed several months of planning. We had to find the right tent to rent or purchase. We had to receive permission from the city council to block off a public area. Tables needed to be purchased, advertising sent out, not to mention acquiring and organizing all the toys and clothing. Nearing the event date, almost all these hurdles had been cleared. The only thing I hadn't anticipated when planning was just how cold it might be outside only one week before Christmas. In fact, that first year we'd had an unusually warm December.

Thank God for His voice! One week from the actual event, I had a dream. I was standing outside the church, near the parking lot. A tent was across the street, but everyone was instead going inside our church building to participate in the giveaway. At first, I was trying to signal everyone they were going to the wrong location, but then I turned to see a giant sign with a digital thermometer. It read 33 degrees Fahrenheit. Then I woke up.

I immediately relayed the dream to our senior leadership team, and after a short deliberation, we agreed it best to heed God's potential warning. With only days to spare, we moved the entire event inside our smaller, but warmer church rental property. We weren't sure it was the right move, but we thought it better to be safe than sorry.

On the day of the event, I woke up early. The doors weren't scheduled to open until 9:00 that morning, and I wasn't sure if many would even come to our outreach. But to my shock, when I looked out the window around 7:30 a.m., there were over 100 people already lined up around the city block! I wept at the sight of it and thanked God for the privilege to serve so many.

Upon closer inspection of the people though, I noticed they were all looking rather uncomfortable. Women's hair tossed in strong gusts of wind. The heat from each person's breath was readily visible in the air. When I looked at the temperature on my phone, it was a frigid 22 degrees Fahrenheit! Had we held the event outdoors all day, the people would have been miserable, including our team! Instead, our team was prepared! My prophetic dream had also sparked the idea to hand out hot chocolate or coffee to those waiting in line.

The event was a major success! After our doors opened, people were able to "shop" until 2 p.m. in the warmth of a heated building. The most incredible part of this story to me, though, is that the average temperature in our town that day ended up being exactly 33 degrees. The God who foreknows all gave us prophetic insight and instruction through a dream. It saved the day for an entire community!

His Voice in Nature

One realm that I struggled in most to believe it could be used by God to speak into my life was nature. It seemed such an ethereal suggestion, at first I dismissed many people's claims to receive prophetic encouragement or guidance through creation. I certainly didn't want to be one of *those* people—you know, the kind who often see clouds in the shapes of angels? And why is it that those people always dye their hair blue?

Nevertheless, God had to tweak my beliefs once more. Upon searching the Scripture more thoroughly on this topic, I was surprised to find His use of creation as an instrument far more prevalent than I had realized. Take the account of Noah, for example.

> [God said,] *"I set My bow in the cloud, and it shall be for a sign of a covenant between Me and the*

earth. It shall come about, when I bring a cloud over the earth, that the bow will be seen in the cloud, and I will remember My covenant" **(Genesis 9:13-14).**

Many of us have grown up reading this portion of Noah's story, but have skimmed over its profundity. The same God, speaking to Noah directly, said He'd also speak to him through nature itself! If Noah could hear God speak so directly, why use nature? The simplest answer is because God chooses to. He's a Creator, after all, and likes to paint with many colors. He authored it all and therefore can speak through it all.

For the anxious longing of the creation waits eagerly for the revealing of the sons of God. ... For we know that the whole creation groans and suffers the pains of childbirth together until now **(Romans 8:19,22).**

Several years ago, my friend Ashley Mele attended a Jesus Culture conference in Chicago, Illinois. When she returned, she told me a nature-related story that humbled my skeptical heart once more. When Ashley was a little girl, she made a regular practice of using her imagination to jump on clouds and slide down rainbows in the sky with Jesus. Of course, most children use their imagination, so her sharing this came as little surprise to me. What Ashley hadn't shared with any human being on the planet, though, was that her practice of sliding down rainbows with Jesus didn't end at childhood. Though she now held a master's degree from a secular university, her childlike faith continually propelled her imagination to play with Jesus in the sky.

Upon returning from the conference in Chicago, Ashley excitedly shared that she'd had an encounter with a man there who prophesied over her about this! As the man at the conference came to the end of his altar ministry with Ashley, he paused as if receiving one last bit of information. He then said, "The Lord loves spending time with you in the sky. He especially loves sliding down rainbows with you."

When Ashley shared this testimony, I stood speechless, humbled, even convicted. Jesus proved that He met with Ashley in the clouds, and I learned that sometimes even the most seemingly childlike things in the natural, God honors as holy!

Jesus said if His people wouldn't praise Him, even the rocks would cry out. The God who is *Logos* (Word) placed *Logos* in all things. When we receive this—when we put faith in the reality that His voice is everywhere and readily accessible—His Word becomes *rhema* (utterance)—ever-present language and life to our starving souls.

To be clear, I'm not suggesting every action in nature is God's voice. I'm also not advocating for seeking signs from the heavens from any other deity or according to any spiritual practice outside of Christ. Rather, what I am declaring is God can and often does use various aspects of creation to communicate His heart, desires, and direction. If only we'd have ears to hear.

The Tone of His Voice

Just as God is not one-dimensional in His ways of communicating, He is not one-dimensional in His emotions. One might even say He has moods. Peace, joy, gentleness, kindness—these are the fruits of His character, the default of His mood. It's not to say He can't be displeased or even angry. Scripture makes clear He has been, at times. However, God is love. Therefore, He majors on the more positive attributes of it.

> *For his anger lasts only a moment, but his favor lasts a lifetime* **(Psalm 30:5).**

One spring day, I was walking through our local park. It was a particularly warm and sunny afternoon, the kind where one might be tempted to fall prey to a nap in the grass. On this day, though, the opposite occurred. My senses opened. Everything seemed louder, brighter, more fulfilling. The birds sang in harmony, the grass appeared painted especially green. Even trees seemed to lift their arms to heaven, waving leafy hands back and forth in worship to God. This may sound as cliché as a cheesy Hallmark movie, but it's truly what I saw.

Without warning, I began to weep. The Holy Spirit overwhelmed me with such revelation of His good nature I had to sit down on the nearest park bench. My sunglasses concealed tears. At the same time, I didn't care if anyone saw my crying. God Almighty was speaking to me about how beautiful His heart was, especially toward us. Sure, the fall of man had produced storms, weeds, and pesky bugs amidst this masterful work, but the original intent was still intact. God's Genesis story was still readily seen in creation's artistry and order.

His Voice Breaks Through

Enemies in our life lurk about. Thorns and thistles sometimes bite our tender flesh. Dark nights of the soul tempt us to despair, and winter seasons chill our bones, yet these temporary, circumstantial flaws ultimately give way to new, hope-filled beauties. The sun always rises and hope really does spring eternal. God reveals His faithfulness, His loving nature in numerous ways again and again. Trials come and go, but Jesus remains constant. When we look through His eyes, listen for His voice, it becomes clear that He is never changing. He is *always* good.

Listen to His wonderful, eclectic voice! It is multi-faceted and manifold in wisdom. His tone is tender. His words are true. He is the God who talks back.

CHAPTER 10

HEALING WITH GOD

"The hole in her heart is gone!" he shouted.

I didn't hear much else after that, at least not the first time around. I was too lost in the moment, somewhere between ecstasy and disbelief. Yet there she stood before us, a young girl of eight years old, miraculously healed.

Hannah Edwards was born with a small defect in her heart, a microscopic hole. She functioned well in her first few months despite it, but in follow-up visits to cardiologists, the condition was deemed degenerative. Surgery to fix the slowly expanding hole was a high risk for an infant, and her parents, Mike and Lisa Edwards, were encouraged to wait until she was old enough to have it safely.

Eight years later, I was leading a young adults group on Sunday nights in my hometown of West Frankfort, Illinois. At 26 years old, I'd grown steadily in the Word, in prayer, and in some of the principles laid out in this book. God had set me on a firm foundation, but I'd yet to see many of the biblical miracles my heart cried out for.

I had seen Christ heal through other ministries, including my father's. I'd been healed myself as a baby (more on that in another chapter), but I'd only personally produced a handful of what you might call "minor" healings through my own ministry. Nevertheless, despite my lack of personal experience, I began regularly teaching on healing via the gospels and the book of Acts.

One night, just a few weeks into the young adults meetings in my hometown, there was a knock at the door. When we opened it, in walked an impressively built blonde man in his 30s, his dark-haired wife, and their young daughter. It was Mike, Lisa, and little Hannah Edwards. I'd never met them, but they'd somehow heard of our group. Mike glanced around the room of 20-somethings before locking eyes with those of us in charge.

Placing his hands upon the back of his young daughter's shoulders, Mike raised his voice, "We've heard this place believes in the power of prayer and healing. Our daughter, Hannah, is two weeks from a major surgery to repair what is now a nickel-sized hole in her heart. The hospital has informed us we must operate now. If we wait much longer Hanna will be at serious risk. But we believe God still heals. Will you pray for her?"

I responded, "Absolutely! Bring her in the center of the living room, and we will all agree in prayer together."

About 15 of us gathered around young Hannah, laying hands upon her in faith. I closed my eyes and with all my heart began to pray, "Jesus, You said in Mark 11:23-24 that if we say to the mountain to be removed and cast into the sea, not doubting in our heart but believing we've already received what we ask, that mountain will obey. In Your ministry, You spoke to sickness, disease, and demons that way. So, we speak to this nickel-sized hole and say, 'In the name of Jesus, be filled! Body, be healed for the glory of God.'"

Others emphatically agreed and we all said "Amen." I remember Mike and Lisa's attitude as being especially joyful. They kindly thanked us, exchanging handshakes and hugs before walking out the door. One week later, we were again having our meeting when the doorbell rang. It was Mike Edwards. I barely greeted him properly before he gleefully started in.

"The hole in her heart is gone! We took Hannah back to St. Louis, Missouri, two days after your Bible study to prep for her surgery on Wednesday. They ran a few standard tests before opening her but couldn't find anything wrong! In fact, the radiologist and surgeon had a bit of an argument over the discrepancy between the X-rays. The one two weeks earlier showed the nickel-sized hole, but the new one showed none! Jesus healed her. Thank you for your prayers."

We were all filled with joy, praising God. I'd been teaching for several years what I knew to be true from the words of Jesus. This was the first time, though, I saw such a major healing through my own prayers!

The testimony spread quickly around our hometown, especially in local church communities. Some cheered. Others jeered. One of our young adults was even scolded by his local pastor for believing in such miracles. Nevertheless, Hannah was healed. I drew a line in the sand in my heart that day. I'd now seen hard evidence for *more,* and no matter the naysaying, no matter the level of opposition, I resolved to pursue the manifest Presence and power of the Holy Spirit until the day I died.

Major Lesson Learned

The principles of kingdom authority and faith for doing the miraculous works of Jesus have continued to bear fruit in my life to this day. I've never forgotten that as little brothers to Christ, we've become His ambassadors. Our mission is to continue Christ's ministry upon the earth. Teaching these truths to others has proven exponentially fruitful, and those who've applied them have often gone from seeing little to no healing to immediate results. That's what happens when we adjust our beliefs to Christ's.

However, I made a critical error in the early days of this miraculous journey. I posited this one truth as the seminal answer for everything. My motives weren't bad, merely misguided. My theology for authority and faith was sound. Hence, the fruit. It just wasn't the full story. That I learned the hard way.

A few months after Hannah's miraculous healing, I decided that it was time a friend of mine paralyzed from the waist down got out of his wheelchair. With my "kingdom authority gun" fully loaded and cocked, I called him up one day and said, "Joey, I have faith God will heal you. I think people have just been praying the wrong way. Will you come to our house church meeting and let me pray for you?"

As it turned out, Joey had been studying the authority of the believer to heal the sick too. Consequently, he'd seen some results in praying for others. So, he not only agreed to my proposal, but he'd already purchased new tennis shoes to walk in when God healed his paralysis. I found this level of faith inspiring. To this day, I still do.

Joey humbly agreed to come a week later to our house meeting with those new shoes in tow. When we arrived that evening, word had already spread that we were going to pray for a fantastic healing. Compassion was abounding. Faith filled the air. All the ingredients for a miracle seemed present.

After a few preliminary greetings, I explained to the group what we were going to do. Many excitedly drew close. Others stood back in a kind of nervous expectation. I asked Joey to wheel to the center of the room where I could place my hands upon his paralyzed limbs. Then, I shouted with great authority, "In the name of Jesus, rise and walk!!" Joey placed his hands upon the sides of his wheelchair and pushed up with his arms. Suspended above the seat of his chair, he tried with all his might to move his legs. Nothing happened. So,

I prayed once more. "In the name of Jesus, I said 'rise and walk!' Feeling come back into these legs, now!"

The room held its breath once more. After a few more moments of fruitless struggle, I looked at everyone and said, "It's okay. We're going to see a miracle today. We will pray until it's done!" This time, with Joey's consent, I grabbed his arms, placed them around my neck and shoulders. His body was now upon my own. I began walking him around the room, step by step, as if he were a giant backpack. His paralyzed legs and feet drug behind us as I shouted, "Be healed! Be healed!"

Several of the women had begun crying at the dramatic scene, but I refused to quit. For half an hour, I continued to drag my friend around that room, shouting and thanking Jesus for the healing. Unfortunately, it never came. We finally both collapsed from exhaustion. The room seemed to grow cold. No one knew what to say or do. In fact, I don't even remember the rest of that night. I'm sure I attempted to placate the crowd with Scriptures of encouragement. Truthfully though, I was dying on the inside.

The next morning, I attempted to reconcile the defeat of our moment. Confusion turned to frustration, then frustration to anger. I yelled at God. "You said this in Your Word! I took an enormous risk. I was willing to embarrass myself for You! Why did You forsake me!? Why did you let us down?"

The heavens seemed silent. I still loved God, but my faith was shaken. Yes, my pride was hurt, but I also felt horrible for Joey. I called and asked his forgiveness for the embarrassing scene. Thankfully, he was gracious and understood that my heart meant well.

After the talk, I ran the scenario over in my mind repeatedly, trying to figure out what could have gone wrong. I reexamined the Scriptures considering that perhaps my more reformed believing friends who'd previously scolded my beliefs were right. Maybe faith had nothing to do with healing. Perhaps it was all according to God's sovereignty. For a season, I almost believed that. But every time I returned to the Scripture, it seemed all too clear: Jesus did not teach that God only desired to heal a select few, and there were far too many verses declaring we played a part in this thing! Stories like the woman with the issue of blood solidified this fact. She sought Jesus out. She touched His garment, not the other way around. Jesus then proclaimed:

> *And He said to her, "Daughter,* ***your faith*** *has made you well; go in peace and be healed of your affliction"* **(Mark 5:34).**

Not only did Jesus attribute the healing to *her* faith, but in Luke's account, Jesus states He didn't even initiate the transfer of anointing and power. Many people were crowded around Him, touching the same garment. Only the woman, though, caused power to go out from Jesus (see Luke 8:45-46)!

What was going on here? If faith worked for her, why did it not work for us with Joey? What was different in our prayers for Hannah that caused her to be healed? No matter how hard I wracked my brain, I could not find "the formula." Thankfully, my love for Jesus was not solely in His healing power.

I loved healing, but I loved God Himself far more. So, with unresolved questions still lingering, I chose to trust Him in the mystery and go on.

A few years passed. Occasional stories of friends being healed helped me overcome the effects of that seeming defeat. I'd nearly forgotten about the incident. The beautiful thing about God, though, is He remembers everything. He knew my soul longed for answers, and He knew exactly how to lead me to better understanding and to work all that had happened in the process for good.

This was the lesson: Principles in God's Word are true, but God is not a formula. He refuses to be relegated merely to one part of His Word. He began explaining to me the missing miracle link—His manifest Presence.

Since that great college-aged revelation, I'd applied abiding in Him to much of my personal relationship with God. The problem was, I'd forgotten to also apply it to His miraculous *works*. The Lord began to explain that He didn't want me to heal for Him. Like everything else I'd learned so far, He wanted me to heal *with* Him! When I more carefully studied the Scripture with this in mind, I saw it!

> *God is spirit, and those who worship Him must worship in spirit and truth* **(John 4:24).**

Spirit and truth. There it was again. In terms of healing, I'd believed much of His truth. Faith was a truth. Authority was a truth. But I'd left out the flip side of the coin! I'd forgotten the Holy Spirit's abiding Presence. In doing so, I'd become deaf to any specific instructions or keys He may want to give to unlock different situations. I had abided with the Spirit in general prayer, but when it came to praying for sickness or deliverance, I'd checked Him at the door. Jesus didn't do that!

> *Therefore Jesus answered and was saying to them, "Truly, truly, I say to you, the Son can do nothing of Himself,* ***unless it is something He sees the Father doing****"* **(John 5:19).**
>
> *You know of Jesus of Nazareth, how God anointed Him with the Holy Spirit and with power, and how He went about doing good and healing all who were oppressed by the devil,* ***for God was with Him*** **(Acts 10:38).**

Then I understood. I needed His abiding Presence as much as I needed authority and faith. I needed His voice. I needed His power and anointing. I'd walked in a measure, but I needed Him to teach me how to better carry and manifest His glory. Thankfully, God was about to rock my world once more, and this time He'd have me pass the point of no return.

CHAPTER 11

CHURCHING WITH GOD

...kindle afresh the gift of God which is in you through the laying on of my hands **(2 Timothy 1:6).**

Sometime after attending Rita Carlton's prayer gathering (the place I'd learned to hear God's voice in long periods of silent prayer), a shift began to occur in the direction of the meetings. We still largely focused on prayer, but we came to the decision to steer the direction more in pursuit of the Presence of the Holy Spirit. One prayer we continued to offer was, "Jesus, we want all You have. We are even willing to lose our reputation in exchange for Your glory."

See, I had tasted enough of the Holy Spirit to know that His miraculous Presence wasn't without some measure of persecution, even from the church. I'd also tasted enough of God's glory to know that being ostracized for it by some was well worth that exchange!

We set our faces like flint. For the next year, we met with one goal: Jesus in the room. Each week, we worshiped. We read Scripture. We prayed. We waited. We took communion. We purposely made room for the Holy Spirit to guide us however He desired. Of course, we weren't perfect in hearing or following Him, but we did our best. Looking back, I realize this was an effective season of training. Many of us were seasoned in the Scriptures, but we were now learning to be led by the Spirit. Over the course of that year, there was a slow and steady increase of the Presence of God with fruit following. Still, we knew there was more.

One day, I was perusing social media when I ran across a shared post from a young man from Nashville, Tennessee. His name was Brent Kelley. In the post, Brent was standing downtown on a street corner, holding a sign that said, "God is love." I clicked on a few more posts and pictures. They were littered with evangelism and balanced scriptural content.

Then, I saw something that really caught my eye. Several young men and women in Brent's photos were lying on their backs in the literal streets of downtown Nashville. A short testimony in one of the photos' captions read, "I was never the same after this night! The Holy Spirit filled me in a way I'd never experienced!" Images like these were similar to what I'd witnessed in college through my own early ministry, but that power had since waned from life. Hungry for the Spirit, I asked Rita's permission to invite Brent to speak at one of our house meetings. She agreed and, to my delight, he scheduled to come just a few weeks later.

The night Brent and his wife, Cessna, walked through the door of Rita's, I knew in my spirit our meetings were about to shift gears. I just didn't realize my entire life would also. Twenty people had gathered to hear what our guest had to say. However, that night Brent didn't teach on miracles, signs, or wonders. Instead, he preached the simple gospel, with an emphasis on the Father's love. Then, Brent transitioned to an invitation. He made a bold and assured statement: "If you want to encounter the tangible love of God, come up here right now."

For a moment, the room was quiet. Finally, one brave soul stepped up, a young woman I'd known for several years. She calmly walked up to Brent without any expression of outward emotion. Everything seemed normal, and much of the room, I'm sure, expected a heartfelt but uneventful moment of prayer. That didn't happen. Brent gently placed his hand upon her shoulder and whispered, "Come, Holy Spirit." A few seconds later, she collapsed on the floor weeping. She then began uncontrollably laughing, as if joy were exuding from the deepest recesses of her soul.

I don't know what everyone else was thinking, but the moment I saw that woman fall to the ground in Jesus' name, I said in my heart, "That's it! I know exactly what that is, and I want it back in my life!" By the time the night had ended, almost the entire group of people were either on the floor or laid back in their chairs encountering the manifest Presence of the Holy Spirit. Jesus had come, and like biblical Jacob who wrestled God, I wasn't planning on letting go of Him until He blessed me with His Presence!

Brent returned several times to Rita's, each time with a crowd of increasing size. The Holy Spirit was faithful to pour out in similar ways each time. We saw many receive Jesus as Lord and Savior for the first time. Others were instantly healed of diseases or had tormenting demons cast out.

Brent and I quickly became like brothers. Our similar passion for Jesus and His power has kept us close in heart to this day. I'm grateful not only for his ministry, but for his unwavering friendship through varying seasons and trials. Both he and Cessna have exceptionally generous and compassionate hearts. I will forever champion their extraordinary call to minister the gospel in power to the nations.

After a few of Rita's meetings, that same Presence and power Brent walked in also began manifesting through the laying on of my hands. Jesus had again anointed me with a greater measure! Consequently, my hunger for prayer increased. I had a renewed passion to win souls and stir revival in the church. I was seeing even more people healed and delivered when I prayed. Others fell, shook, and were filled with the fire of the Holy Ghost, many never to be the same.

Backlash

I've learned something about the glory of God. Almost all Christians agree with it in principle and in prayer. That is, until it comes. When His Presence and power actually begin to manifest, then you find out who means those prayers. Some joyfully receive Him, submitting to His ways. Others reveal they only want the measure of God they can have and still maintain control over their own lives and church meetings.

Initially, reports of the miracles at Rita's meetings caused ecstatic praise. Then, a backlash came. Rumors spread. Words and actions were twisted. Contexts were removed. Some men and women even later admitted to me personally that they'd become jealous of the power they saw us walking in. They stirred up much of the community against us. Some said we were arrogant while others said we had demons.

Unfortunately, this pressure upon Rita to navigate the varying opinions was only made worse by the fact the crowds were quickly outgrowing the size of her delicate living room. Her yard was often damaged by vehicles parking carelessly on the property. Change was needed, so an agreement for some of us to transition to a new location was made. Rita blessed us and we stepped out into a new season.

Lofty New Beginnings

By this time, God had blessed me with a large loft space in downtown Herrin, Illinois. Though it had only two bedrooms and one bath, the rest of the place was an open floor plan with 18-foot ceilings. It would certainly be a spatial upgrade from Rita's house, and with ceilings that tall, talk about natural vocal reverb!

We decided to give the loft a go. Hours before the first meeting, though, I was suddenly hit with trepidation. I realized these meetings were no longer another person's responsibility. At Rita's there were always several in authority. We navigated things together. Now, this was *my* house. The buck would stop with me. As a result, 30 minutes before our first night meeting, I would be found lying in a fetal position on my bedroom floor, fighting doubts God would even show up. My thoughts raced: *People are coming to encounter the supernatural here. What if that all stayed behind at the other place? Would God continue to back me? Would people even show up?"*

At 6 p.m. on a Tuesday, I finally picked myself up off the beige bedroom carpet. I brushed the lint off the only dress shirt I owned and made my way into the living room. Seven people were waiting for me. Concealing beads of nervous sweat dripping down my back, I grabbed the guitar and began leading the group in worship. We then had a time of silent prayer followed by testimonies and teaching. The overall atmosphere felt peaceful, and the people were smiling. Finally came the time we usually set aside for praying for people's needs.

One woman asked us to lay hands upon her. I cannot recall what her particular need was, but I do remember that when we prayed, the Holy Spirit's Presence came upon her in the same way we'd grown accustomed to at our meetings at Rita's. The woman experienced the tangible weight and joy of the Lord. She laughed, jumped up and down, and shouted, "Thank You, Jesus!"

Eight people came to that first meeting in my loft, and so did God! The King of the universe had chosen to honor us with His Presence once more.

Five months later, over 90 people were packing into my two-bedroom apartment to meet with the living Jesus. The sound of the worship reverberated through the walls and was said to be heard up to a block away. In those short months, drug addicts had been saved and baptized in water. Broken arms, backs, and even some internal issues were instantly healed. Demons regularly manifested and were cast out. The Holy Spirit's power and love had put so many on the floor, we had to buy a bigger rug for their bodies to fall upon softly.

> *When Jesus said to them, "I am," they drew back and fell to the ground* **(John 18:6 NCB).**

The revelation of working *with* God had now begun to encompass every facet of my life. Biblical principles of authority and faith were only part of the story. The Holy Spirit's leadership and anointing were the other. *Anointing* in the original New Testament Greek carries several connotations, but arguably the most prominent simply means "to be smeared with God." See, we aren't to pray for others merely from a catalogue of memorized Scriptures, but with the Presence of God simultaneously oozing from our very beings. This is the two-sided coin of kingdom living—as we abide in Jesus, He will be at work in and through us at all times.

Over the years, some have asked, "Isn't praying for miracles a selfish endeavor?" On the contrary, Jesus proclaims when we receive answers to prayer, God is even more glorified!

If you abide in Me, and My words abide in you, ask whatever you wish, and it will be done for you. My Father is glorified by this, that you bear much fruit, and so prove to be My disciples **(John 15:7-8).**

Noted Healing Miracles

To the glory of Christ, we have now seen more healings in our church services than I can count. That is not to say we have seen everyone 100 percent healed instantly, but since adopting a Spirit and truth approach, we have seen an exponential increase in the frequency and intensity of miracles. As we continue to abide in His Presence and truth, He takes us from glory to increasing glory (see 2 Cor. 3:17-18).

One such noted healing in our church involved a woman from Indiana. Her backstory was one of terrible rejection, brokenness, and abuse. She'd heard about our church through word of mouth and came seeking emotional healing. Little did she know, she would receive a system-wide overhaul from heaven!

There were three of us ministering that day—Donna Colson, Lydia Imhoff, and me. Typically, we'd begin a session by carefully listening to the person's backstory and asking Spirit-led questions along the way. This time, though, the three of us felt led to immediately ask the woman if she'd been born again. When she replied, "No," we knew this was the best place to start.

We shared the gospel with the woman—that God so valued and loved her, He gave His Son that she could be set totally free and start fresh with a new identity and relationship with Him. She replied that she'd never heard about Jesus in such ways. Donna prayed with her, and she willingly repented and received Christ into her life. Immediately, the woman began to feel what she described as tangible waves of peace flooding over her soul and body. God was just getting started though!

Donna then asked about a wrist brace upon her arm. The woman shared with us that she'd recently been in a roll-over ATV accident and had broken her wrist so badly she required heavy pain medication to even function. She showed us a picture of the bone nearly protruding through the skin the night before. We then laid hands upon the wrist and prayed. On a pain scale from 10 to 0, the woman's pain level went from an 8 to a 0 so quickly, her eyes widened in shock. She removed the brace and began to pick up heavy objects while tears of joy streamed down her face!

"I couldn't even feed myself!" she exclaimed. "Now I can painlessly lift a chair with this arm!"

When we gently laid hands on the woman again, the Holy Spirit came upon her, and her body began to shake. She'd never seen nor heard of such a thing, but began shouting, "This is real!" Suddenly, her English supernaturally changed to a language she'd never spoken before as the Spirit surged through her with waves of love. Lydia then gave her a prophetic word that "God was going to restore the joy of sand beneath her feet." To everyone's awe, the woman shared how she'd served in the Middle East during her time in the military, and that because of the horrific things she saw, she'd not set foot on beach sand since.

Finally understanding that Jesus wanted to redeem every aspect of her life, the woman informed us of an autoimmune disease she'd been diagnosed with that rendered her legally blind in the right eye. At this point, I felt led to walk her through a few prayers of forgiveness for those who'd hurt her in the past. I also had her forgive herself, as Christ had forgiven her. She did so willingly, and when we prayed for her blind eye, it opened completely! To confirm, we had her perform a reading test with her healthy eye covered. She read the notes from my phone at a great distance!

How God desires to heal every broken part! This woman came seeking emotional healing. Instead, she was eternally saved, physically healed of a myriad of issues, accurately received prophetic promises, and was baptized in the Holy Spirit! She once was blind, but now could see—in every sense of the phrase.

Groucho Marx

Sometimes, God reveals His humor in a miracle. Just before the beginning of one of our Sunday night services, my associate pastor, Carl Hosick, whispered to me, "Do you know who Groucho Marx is?"

I responded, "I think so. The old film actor with the iconic mustache and glasses, right?"

Being near the computer in the back of the sanctuary, we began pulling up any information we could on the actor from Google's search engine. While doing so, Carl continued, "On the way to church tonight, I was asking God to speak to me about anyone he might want to minister to. A few seconds later, I saw a picture in my mind of Groucho Marx. I'm only vaguely familiar with who that is, but it was so random I thought there was a good chance it was the Holy Spirit."

Only a few minutes after our discussion, a first-time visitor to the church walked in. He was an older gentleman with very distinct facial features. He wore round glasses and bore a large, fuzzy mustache almost identical to that of Groucho Marx! Knowing this was likely no coincidence, Carl made his way over to introduce himself to the man. His name was Charlie. He was a former police officer from Chicago, Illinois.

Carl asked, "I know this might sound crazy, but I saw an image of a man just like you before coming to church tonight. Is there anything you need prayer for?"

At first, Charlie hesitated to think of anything specific. Suddenly though, he realized long-standing conditions applied! As it turned out, for 48 years, Charlie had dealt with hearing loss. Even with the use of modern aids (which he was wearing upon entry to our church service), Charlie had to focus carefully on people's lips. But Carl believed the Holy Spirit wanted to heal him. Laying his hands upon Charlie's ears, Carl said authoritatively, "In the name of Jesus, deafness leave. Hearing be restored, right now!"

Charlie's eyes widened. With hearing aids still in, his ears were suddenly flooded with an unbearable volume of sound. He then removed the devices. Carl tested the accuracy of his hearing by whispering the name of Jesus from a distance and direction Charlie could not previously hear or see. Tears filled Charlie's eyes. God did it! After nearly a half century, his hearing was perfectly restored. Charlie left that night with hearing aids in his pockets, and a broad smile beneath the white, fluffy mustache on his face.

Bullet List of Healings

It would be impossible for me to recall every healing miracle we've seen in this outpouring thus far. To say I'm grateful to Jesus for that is an understatement. He is worthy of all glory and praise, but so that you may believe He is still willing to stretch forth His hand in our day, here is an alphabetical bullet list of conditions I can recall with certainty being healed:

- ADHD
- Aortic/heart valve condition
- Asthma
- Arthritis
- Autoimmune diseases (various)
- Bacterial infections
- Blindness (partial/total)
- Blood disorders (various)

- Bronchitis
- Broken bones
- Cancer (various)
- Carpel tunnel syndrome
- Chronic pain (bones/muscles/nerves)
- Common cold
- COVID-19
- Crohn's Disease
- Deafness (partial and total)
- Diabetes
- Ear infections
- Falls (complications from)
- Fibromyalgia
- Genetic disorders
- Genital herpes
- Hepatitis
- Hypertension
- IBS/IBD
- Infertility
- Influenza
- Kidney diseases
- Latex allergies
- Leg lengths/hip alignment
- Lockjaw

- Lupus
- Mental Health (various)
- Muteness (unable to speak)
- Nutritional deficiencies
- Ovarian cysts
- Pregnancy complications
- Psoriasis
- Rheumatoid arthritis
- Scoliosis
- Seizure disorders
- Sleep disorders
- Thyroid disorders
- Tuberculosis
- Viral infections
- Women's bleeding disorders

The Holy Spirit's Presence is what's missing from much of the church, but when and where He's allowed to move, the same works Jesus did in the gospels happen today. If there are mysteries, they are invitations to be explored. I'm not suggesting I personally have or will unlock every mystery of sickness or disease yet to be healed, but I am saying the default position of Christ on this matter was made clear 2,000 years ago.

> *This was to fulfill what was spoken through Isaiah the prophet: "He Himself took our infirmities and*

> *carried away our diseases"* **(Matthew 8:17; see also Isaiah 53:4).**

This is how the first church believed (see James 5:14-16). They did not beg God to heal anyone. Most of them had already been commissioned by Jesus personally to go into every town and village to heal, and that was before His crucifixion, resurrection, and ascension! Perhaps this is why Peter later states with confidence that the power to heal He already possessed within (via Christ).

> *Peter said, "I do not possess silver and gold, but what I do have I give to you: In the name of Jesus Christ the Nazarene—walk!" And seizing him by the right hand, he raised him up; and immediately his feet and his ankles were strengthened* **(Acts 3:6-7).**

If we will merely humble ourselves, align to Christ's teachings, and relationally abide in His Spirit, He will cause us to bear much fruit—including His work of redemptive healing upon the earth!

Casting Out Demons

Sometimes sickness is connected to demonization (Luke 13:16; Mark 9:25; Matt. 17:15-21). I don't believe there is a demon under every rock, but I can now tell you with certainty, they're under far more rocks than most people are aware! While the Bible is clear that human flesh has its role in sin and earthly strife, many don't realize the level to which the demonic is at work amidst that sin. Demons feed off the fruits of flesh. They are empowered by it, capitalizing on the effects of sin on the earth.

> *Our struggle is not against flesh and blood* **(Ephesians 6:12).**

Before I received an increase of the Presence of the Holy Spirit and learned to abide in Him, I'd only seen two or three demons in my entire life. After that increase came, though, they would manifest often in our meetings and even sometimes on the streets as I'd walk by. Demons can stay hidden when the anointing isn't present, and so they often do. But the manifest Presence of God draws them out! This certainly was the case in Jesus' ministry.

> *Just then there was a man in their synagogue with an unclean spirit...And Jesus rebuked him, saying, "Be quiet, and come out of him!" Throwing him into convulsions, the unclean spirit cried out with a loud voice and came out of him* **(Mark 1:23,25-26).**

A lot of people have the idea that demons are rare, or perhaps relegated to a third-world country somewhere, where people sacrifice directly to the devil. Well, demons are certainly in those places, but this passage is the very first mention of demonic deliverance in the gospels, and it took place in a synagogue—basically a Jewish church!

When the Spirit began to fall in our meetings, we'd sometimes have people falling on the floor and manifesting devils during worship. No one would even lay hands on them. Just the atmosphere of heaven in the room caused them to surface. Other times, during the preaching, demonic spirits would cause people to become disruptive. Other people under the influence of demons would literally run out of our doors having panic attacks or sudden migraine headaches.

We now know how to better deal with these dark influences, often resulting in freedom for the person who is demonized. It was a learning curve, though, for sure. I do not have sufficient time or space to provide an extensive teaching on demons and deliverance in this book, but I will cover some of the more prominent points of significance for this chapter. Otherwise, there are many insightful books written more specifically on the subject. For those interested, I would personally recommend a ministry friend of mine named Jake Kail, who has written several biblically based books on demons including *Setting Captives Free*.

It's Worth Mentioning

Demons often enter people through "doors" such as fear, abuse, sexual sin, excessive anger, bitterness, unforgiveness, and more. They can also attempt to follow generational bloodlines. Others are acquired through participation—whether willful or in ignorance—with witchcraft or the occult.

Now, some demons come out very easily. They can leave through water baptism, in a moment of Presence-centered worship, through an authoritative command, or even a hug given in agape love. We've personally seen all these types of deliverances. Other demons are more stubborn, or more deeply embedded in the soul of a person. The latter can occur as people open various layers of their being to the devil through traumatic experiences, repeated acts of sin, or direct engagement with witchcraft.

Unfortunately, many in our culture aren't aware that some activities our western society deems as normal are wrought with demonic mysticism and idolatrous practices. We've cast demons out of people who have engaged with psychics, fortune-tellers, and various astrologers. Practices such as reiki, acupuncture, and kundalini have also resulted in demons manifesting in our meetings. We've even cast spirits out of people who've done yoga. Some readers may scoff at that, but it's not a suggestion. I'm telling you it's happened many times! I can introduce you to some of the people who have been set free.

Many Americans view these new-age practices as harmless, yet they have roots in and ties to eastern religions. Yoga, in particular, which literally means "to yoke" or "to unite," is not merely an act of physically stretching. Many of the positions themselves are worship poses to idols or foreign gods.

> *No, but I say that the things which the Gentiles sacrifice, they sacrifice to demons and not to God; and I do not want you to become sharers in demons* **(1 Corinthians 10:20).**

You might say, "Well, that's not my intention," but the devil doesn't care. God may not be angry if your motives are pure, but the devil doesn't play fair. If a child innocently plays with a snake, the parent may not be angry with them for it, but that doesn't mean the snake won't bite. This is how the kingdom of darkness often harms us through ignorance.

How Can Christians Have Demons?

This is likely the most common question asked concerning deliverance. Many say, "I was taught the devil can't be in the same place as Holy God."

Well, you were taught wrong. I was too at one point. Even in the Old Testament, we see satan sometimes appearing directly in the Holy Presence of Almighty God (see Job 1–2). Before the very last day, when death is put under Christ's feet and all is handed over to the Father (see 1 Cor. 15:25-28), God and the demonic can exist in the same vicinity. The church is to be the army of God, ambassadors of heaven in the midst of a spiritual war on earth. An example of the early battlefield between God and evil would be the Jewish temple.

The Jewish temple generally consisted of three parts: the Holy of Holies, the inner court, and the outer court. The temple itself is a prophetic shadow of what God intended after Christ, which was to put His Holy Presence inside of human beings. However, in Jesus' day, thieves often resided within the inner and outer courts of the temple.

> *And within the temple grounds He found those who were selling oxen, sheep, and doves, and*

the money changers seated at their tables. And He made a whip of cords, and drove them all out of the temple area, with the sheep and the oxen; and He poured out the coins of the money changers and overturned their tables; and to those who were selling the doves He said, "Take these things away from here; stop making My Father's house a place of business!" His disciples remembered that it was written: "Zeal for Your house will consume me" **(John 2:14-17 NASB).**

Jesus was so furious to find God's holy temple infested with thieves, He flipped over tables and ran them out with a whip! Today, God's human temples (Christians) also consist of three parts: spirit, soul, and body (see 1 Thess. 5:23). While our human spirits are immediately sanctified/perfected at new birth (see Col. 1:22; Eph. 4:24-25), demonic thieves can occupy our still-in-process souls and bodies. They enter through "open doors" either directly in the person's life or via generational iniquities. Jesus wants to drive these thieves out!

See, God presided over Israel as His sovereignly chosen people, but demons (and sickness) still ran rampant in His camp until the Anointed One came into direct contact. When Jesus, smeared with God's power, came near, dark powers scattered (see Act 10:38). So, sovereign or omnipresent proximity isn't God's best. Manifest proximity is! The Holy Spirit is vital, and that's why the devil fights hard to keep our relationship with Him dull. He will even use misguided theology to do it. If satan can keep Christians from engaging the anointing of the Spirit, he can keep their inner and outer courts demonized. In this case, updating your understanding of the kingdom of God may just change your life!

Jesus Is the Best Deliverance Minister

One of the chief lessons of working with God in deliverance is that there are no formulas. Applicable principles about overcoming the kingdom of darkness are certainly within Scripture, but the moment we adopt blanket methodologies for casting out demons, we remove much of the partnership God wants to play in the process.

Now, God did not promise that He would always do what I'm about to share in this last story. But He didn't promise He wouldn't. Out of the hundreds upon hundreds of deliverances we've seen thus far in our ministry, the instance that stands out above all others in my mind is when Jesus Himself showed up to finish the job. This time, I don't mean the Holy Spirit. I mean the Son of God Himself!

It was yet another Sunday evening, this time toward the end of the service. Many people had been prayed for, and the Holy Spirit had moved upon them powerfully. A time of spontaneous worship had erupted among those still lingering. On the far end of the front altar area, I noticed a young girl leaning against the wall. She didn't seem to have the same peace as the others. In fact, she was acting aloof, with an almost blank expression upon her face.

I grabbed a female leader, and we made our way over to her to calmly investigate. When we placed our hands upon the girl, she suddenly fell to the floor and began thrashing about, manifesting demons. Now, normally a demon either leaves quickly, or deeper heart issues need to be addressed to get to the root of the stronghold.

This time, however, as we ministered, another demon surfaced. Then another, and another. After just a few minutes, it was evident this girl was overcome by countless spirits, and with the unveiling of each one came an even greater violence. We took authority over any physical harm the demons might try to inflict, and it did prevent them from injuring her externally, but the girl was still tormented internally.

The Holy Spirit gave several of us words of knowledge revealing a few key evil spirits. We prayed and they would leave, but there were so many others manifesting, we knew this was going to take a while apart from some special divine intervention.

The problem was, we'd already been in service for five hours and those few of us remaining were tired. We weren't sure we had physical stamina to go all night. We didn't want to put the exhausted girl through that type of marathon either. The demons continued to manifest with great ferocity. The girl's eyes were rolling around in her head as she thrashed about undergoing torment by her invisible captors.

Meanwhile, I had a personal problem. I *really* had to pee. My bladder was so full I was in pain! I whispered to the woman next to me to keep an eye on the girl. Then I practically ran to the restroom. After washing my hands, I looked into the mirror and had an honest conversation with God.

"Lord, You've allowed us to cast out many demons. You know we've always tried to work with You, and You've always been faithful. But right now, I'm at a loss. I don't know what else to do with this girl. Besides that, I'm exhausted. Jesus, help."

When I came out of the restroom, the girl was still thrashing and screaming, except now, one of our stronger prophetic people, Jeremy Mitchell, was sitting nearby on the edge of our stage, staring intently at her. You could see the wheels turning in his head.

I stepped over and humbly asked, "What do you think? Are you seeing something?"

He gently responded, "She's in a large room, trying to reach for the door, but a mob of demons keep pulling her back in. She needs someone to pull her out of that room."

Large room? In the natural the only large room this girl was in was our sanctuary. Jeremy was talking about an invisible room that apparently only he could see. If I were going to concede this prophetic word as accurate, I'd have to really go out on the limb of faith. An invisible demon room? Where is that in the Bible? Then again, we were desperate. Nothing we'd done had worked. Besides that, Jeremy wasn't known for flighty prophecies about blue unicorns flying in cotton candy clouds. Not to say that wouldn't be interesting.

We had nothing left to lose. So, I prayed aloud, "Jesus, would You personally come and pull her out of that room?"

Seconds later, the girl gasped, her eyes opened wide, and she became fully coherent. Screaming with joy, she exclaimed, "Did you see Him!? Did you see Him!? He was right here!"

"Did we see who?" I calmly asked.

With her facial expression suggesting I was the one talking crazy, she emphatically replied, "Jesus was just here! Jesus! How could you not see Him? He was right here!"

Tears fell from her eyes onto the floor she had thrashed about only moments ago. "You missed Him! You missed Him," she repeated hysterically between breaths.

After a few moments, we were able to calm the young girl down enough to hear the rest of her story. She described how she was in a dark jail cell, surrounded by creatures cursing her. She felt excruciating pain as they tore at her limbs. One, she said, even tried jumping down her throat. This made sense as, at times in the natural, she would suddenly make gagging sounds while on the floor.

Suddenly, a bright light appeared in the jail cell. An authoritative, masculine voice yelled, "Let her go!" It was Jesus Christ! He grabbed her hand and yanked her from the demons' grasp. They all shrieked in terror at the sight of His glory. Jesus then said to the girl, "Daughter, you are free. Your brothers and sisters are waiting for you. They didn't give up. Tell them I'm so proud of them and know that I love you and forgive you of sin."

We were in awe. In an instant, this young girl had gone from hellish torment to total peace. We found out later that she had been wickedly abused as a young girl by a babysitter. The older woman would take her in the basement and perform unspeakable, satanic acts over her. Now, though, she was in her right mind. Not only that, but something else had changed. Before her deliverance, this girl was very timid around people in our church. Now, she was practically glowing, enthusiastically hugging everyone, as if she didn't have a care in the world. I have rarely met anyone filled with such peace and joy. That's what happens when we behold our King. We are transformed into the image of His glory.

CHAPTER 12

HARVESTING WITH GOD

The miracles we were seeing in our Loft Church services were beautiful. Christians were falling even more in love with Jesus as He loved them and set them free from the effects of sin and death. What about the world, though? Would God do similar works among the unsaved?

I grew up hearing the world was ending at any minute. Jesus was to rescue us from the certain Armageddon I was told would take place after each Middle Eastern skirmish. Of course, it didn't happen. Preachers sold a lot of books and sermon series on CD, but we were still here.

That's when I decided to study the Scriptures more thoroughly for myself. What I discovered was largely a different paradigm. Although I believe the Bible is clear that Jesus will return and the world will ultimately be judged for sin, the full counsel of the New Testament makes a compelling case for the kingdom of God continually advancing in the earth in great glory. In this, the power of the Holy Spirit isn't an escape hatch to rescue the church from a sinful world, but a Personal force of love to rescue a sinful world from the power of the devil! In other words, the church is not my mission field, my mission field is the world!

> *And He said to them, "Go into all the world and preach the gospel to all creation. ...These* [miraculous] *signs will accompany those who have believed"* **(Mark 16:15,17).**

Now convinced we weren't to be obsessing over the end of the world, I stopped hiding. I stopped viewing everyone as evil, untouchable, to be boycotted. After all, it's hard to love someone you think should be "left behind." Instead, I began seeing the lost as candidates for grace, to be reconciled to a God who so passionately loved them, He died to prove it. I started seeking after them, according to the model Christ revealed in the gospels.

My friend and powerful evangelist Shawn Hurley once profoundly summarized it like this, "Theology is knowing what God would do. Love is doing it."

Now, the message of the gospel still requires repentance. It still demands a total surrender to the Lordship of Jesus Christ. But we must be sure to never conflate God's feelings about sin itself with His feelings about sinful humanity. One He abhors; the other He adores.

God is a loving Father, desiring that none of His creation perish (see 2 Pet. 3:9). Likewise, I'm not here to curse a darkened people. I'm here to show a darkened people God's light. I'm not here to call down fire upon sinners. I'm here to show those who sin salvation. I'm not calling for the world to burn. I'm burning to call the world to Christ.

> *For behold, darkness will cover the earth and deep darkness the peoples; but the Lord will rise upon you and His glory will appear upon you. Nations will come to your light, and kings to the brightness of your rising* **(Isaiah 60:2-3).**

When I quit viewing the world as my enemy and instead began to seek after the very ones religion told me to avoid, the power of the Holy Spirit began to manifest regularly. Miracles backed the message I preached. Rather than one salvation a year, I began seeing hundreds. Then, thousands!

Again, I'm not suggesting Jesus doesn't have fire in His eyes. He is the King of Glory, to be deeply revered. People need to confess and deal with their sins. All of that is true. However, they come to that place of repentance and the knowledge of the truth by love.

> *The goodness of God leads you to repentance* **(Romans 2:4 NKJV).**

Therefore, I'll leave the end-times debates to others. I'm no universalist, but whether it's pre-trib, post-trib, or Jesus returns eating a prime rib, I can't say with certainty. What I can say, though, is this: When I stopped boycotting the world for seemingly loving hell and instead began loving the hell out of the world, God began working with me in spreading the good news. He backed me up with miraculous Presence and power.

Dillards

The first few months after Loft Church started, I was still working full time in the men's suit department of Dillards. Since starting the job, Jesus had allowed me to minister to several in the area of healing specifically. One of my managers had a sprained knee, for example, and was healed instantly. He reported back to the rest of the office staff, "I'd never seen a true miracle in my life until today, and it happened to me!"

Because of the authority and weight this manager carried with the rest of the staff, a funny rumor began to spread about me throughout the store. Many didn't really understand the gospel, so they said, "Josh has healing powers." I would, of course, give Jesus the praise every chance I could, but with some it didn't matter. Several of my coworkers seemed to get it, but others more unfamiliar with the supernatural began avoiding me like the plague.

Most of the people God had touched were spread throughout various departments within our store. Ironically though, the men's clothing area where I worked had been the least to encounter God. So, they were among the most skeptical. The lady who worked two sections down from me, Rene, had a rather scoffing attitude toward my *other* job as a minister. In fact, she would address me as "reverend" each time I would pass by her station. Sure, she had a smile on her face, but we all knew there was a measure of mocking behind it. I did my best to just laugh along with her, opting for self-deprecating humor rather than offense.

Strike one.

On the opposite side of the men's department was a man named Bill, who was in his late 40s and homosexual. He had been with our store for so long, he was well known throughout the community. Now, I'm normally not one to be intimidated by people, but Bill was an exception. It wasn't his sexual orientation that caused me hesitation so much as his caustic wit. Also, he was very jaded by the Catholic religion in which he grew up. I didn't know exactly what had happened to him, but I knew it didn't produce fond feelings toward God or those claiming to know Him. As such, Bill made clear he did not think highly of me either. Despite my best efforts to thwart his stereotyping, to him I still seemed yet another young, uninformed Bible-belter, thumping my self-righteous views upon everyone.

Strike two.

Finally, the woman who worked directly to my left in shoes, Theresa, seemed the more cordial of the three. She was a single mom and a diligent worker, but it didn't take much discernment to recognize she wasn't in love with her job. Her smiling interactions toward me seemed little more than a plastic façade also. To add insult to injury, she was a good friend of the first woman, Rene, and a few times I had even overheard them making cracks about me under their breath.

I would be lying if I said coming into this situation every day was easy. Nevertheless, I did my best to keep my head down and work diligently with a good attitude. What they didn't know was I would often pray for hours to God throughout my shift. Sometimes, I would even sneak off for a few minutes into the dressing rooms to do so—but let's pretend you didn't hear that from me. In seriousness, my heart was crying out for the salvation of those in my department. But opportunities to minister to them continued to be scarce. Sure, I could be brash and just hammer them with a heaven or hell ultimatum, but while that may be applicable at times, I sensed that approach wouldn't bode well with my coworkers.

So, I worked. I waited. Then, one day the opportunity came.

I had clocked in and just begun my shift as usual in the men's suit department when I suddenly saw Theresa, from women's shoes, bent over and slowly hobbling to her workstation. Not only did she look to be in pain, but she was literally wincing with every excruciating step.

Before I could walk over to ask if she was okay, the other woman in my department, Rene, did so. I watched as she helped Theresa to carefully sit down. Pretending not to eavesdrop, I overheard Rene ask, "Why are you here? You're in no shape to work!" Theresa responded, "I have to. We are tight this month, and if I don't work every shift, I won't be able to pay the bills and feed my daughter."

My heart broke. I knew this was an opportunity to demonstrate the love of Jesus, but I also knew if I fouled up such a vulnerable moment, I'd never get another chance to share with any of them. For a few moments, I slipped away once more to the dressing rooms and prayed. "God, You have not given me a spirit of fear. Your Word says instead that I am a partaker of Your divine nature (see 2 Pet. 1:4), and if I lay hands on the sick, they shall recover (see Mark 16:17). So, I'm going out there and doing this for the sake of Your glory. Thank You for being with me."

I've learned something in my years of evangelism: There's a time to back off, but sometimes you just have to look your frightened flesh square in the eye and say, "You don't get a say today. We are doing the opposite!"

I walked out of the dressing room and straight up to Theresa. She was sitting down on a bench, still grimacing from her pain. I said to her, "I'm so sorry you're hurting. Can I ask what happened?"

Through painfully gritted teeth she responded, "I slipped in my shower and fell directly on my tailbone this morning. I can't even stand straight up. The pain is horrendous."

Not wanting to abuse her time, I just came out with it. "You've got to let me pray for you," I said. "What do you have to lose?"

Theresa hesitated, before reluctantly responding, "Okay."

I placed one hand on the middle of her back and one upon her shoulder. Then, I boldly said, "I command anything broken, torn, or bruised to be healed now, in the name of Jesus. Pain, get out of this body. Holy Spirit, come."

Suddenly, Theresa's eyes widened. She took a deep breath. A few moments later, her hands began frantically fanning her sweat-laden face.

"What is happening?" she exclaimed. "I feel a sudden heat coming all over me!"

No more than 15 seconds later, Theresa sat up perfectly straight with no pain. She looked up at me in shock. "What did you do? It's gone!"

I replied, "I just prayed for you. Jesus healed your back, because He loves you so much."

She then stood up and walked a few feet before bursting into loud sobs of gratitude. At that moment, our co-worker, Rene, walked over to investigate the commotion. When she saw Theresa walking upright, she looked worried and asked, "What is going on? Are you okay?"

When Theresa relayed the events, Rene took one step back, looked at Theresa, then looked at me, and stormed off in the other direction. I don't know if she was angry or freaked out. Either way, there was nothing she could say. There's something about miracles that tends to supersede most disagreements or debates. I was reminded in that moment of this Scripture:

> *And seeing the man who had been healed standing with them, they* [Peter and John's accusers] *had nothing to say in reply* **(Acts 4:14).**

For the next few minutes, I shared the gospel with Theresa. I told her that the God of the universe was madly in love with her and demonstrated that love through the cross. He only further proved it by healing her body when another one of His kids prayed. She began crying. She'd only previously known legalistic religion, but now wanted to know Jesus as Lord.

Elated, I walked back to my department. But God wasn't done yet! Theresa, now pain-free and newly flooded with Christ's love, took Rene to lunch that day. When they returned, Theresa motioned me over, "Rene sent me a text that I wanted you to see. Don't let her know I showed you, but you should know...."

She took out her phone and read Rene's words, "I have always struggled with God and religion. But I think he [meaning me] just made a believer out of two unbelievers."

The day before these events, I thought I'd nearly struck out with all three of my coworkers. Yet, in one moment, the Lord reversed the count. Debate could not have moved hearts like this. There's a time for speech and the influence of minds, but it's the demonstration of the Spirit and power that draws people's hearts. It is the better way!

> *My message and my preaching were not with wise and persuasive words* [of human reasoning], *but with a demonstration of the Spirit's power, so that your faith might not rest on human wisdom, but on God's power* **(1 Corinthians 2:4-6 NIV).**

I left work that night on cloud nine. Still, in the back of my mind, I wondered about Bill. He was so hardened. Could God reach him too? It seemed impossible in the natural, but then, I had just seen God do the impossible.

God Breaks Out in School

A few weeks after Theresa's healing in Dillards, I felt a strong impression from the Lord to take a step of faith into full-time ministry. Loft Church was reaching the point of needing my full attention, and although we never asked for money, God had been faithful to bring in enough donations to pay every bill and then some. Several people at the church wanted to support me of their own volition also.

So, after over 20 years of working secular jobs, I took the leap fully into the Father's arms. The only downside to handing in my two weeks' notice at Dillards was I'd yet to have an opportunity with Bill. He still seemed as acid-tongued as ever, and I knew if his heart were to be moved by God, it would take something substantial.

One week before my retail-life exit, I was scheduled to speak at a morning chapel for a local Christian school. I'd done this chapel service for several years in a row. Before their first classes, approximately 500 elementary students would gather in the bleachers of their gymnasium for a short Bible lesson and prayer. Each year I came, the teachers asked me to play guitar and sing for the kids. This year, though, they'd given me free rein to speak to them about anything I'd like.

The chapel service only lasted about 20 minutes, so I knew I would need to be succinct. I felt led to speak to them about walking a life of miracles with Christ. For about 15 minutes, I poured into those kids relevant Scripture and recent testimonies of God healing the sick. At the end, I gave an invitation to anyone desiring to live a surrendered life to Christ. Almost every single hand in the building went up! Then, with permission of the administration, I invited anyone who needed individual prayer to form a short line in front of me. I expected no more than three to four kids to come forward, but to my shock, the line nearly extended out of the gymnasium!

The first girl who asked for prayer had a sprained wrist. I knew if I was going to get through this line, I'd need to pray quickly, so I simply laid hands on her and said, "Be healed, in Jesus' name." When the girl checked for the pain, she screamed, "It's healed! I have no pain!" She took her wrist brace off and showed everyone. Now, even more kids were getting in line, and one after one, God healed them all. To my memory, not a single child went without a miracle of some kind! In fact, so many kids were being touched by God, the principal made a special announcement they were going to postpone their first hour of classes!

To conserve time, I began instructing the teachers how to pray with authority. At first, several were timid and reverted to "begging" prayers. The healings dried up immediately. So, I took them to Mark 11:23-24 and instructed that Jesus was the one who taught this type of prayer regarding sickness and demons. Two of the teachers seemed to believe and consequently altered the way they prayed. Guess what? The kids began receiving healing from those two teachers!

Finally, one young man about the age of 10 years old timidly stepped forward. The boy was chubby, wore a horizontally striped yellow and white polo and had "coke-bottle" glasses. That is to say, the lenses on the glasses were so thick, his eyeballs looked enormously magnified. I leaned down and whispered to the boy, "What can I pray for, my man?"

He gently replied, "I want to see perfectly. I don't want to wear these glasses anymore."

"Okay, son," I said. "Let's do a before test so that we can truly confirm when God heals you. Go ahead and remove your glasses."

I took my cell phone from my right pocket and quickly typed up a small note. Then, I stood back 10 feet or so and asked the boy to read what I'd written. He couldn't make out a single letter. I stepped five feet closer and we tried again. Still blind as a bat! Although I'd just seen scores of children healed of every external condition you could think of, suddenly my carnal mind began doubting. I was like Peter who walked on water until he began focusing more on the strength of the opposing wind and waves. Something about those glasses rattled my faith cage.

Thankfully, this wasn't my first rodeo with the voice of doubt. I ordered my internal thoughts to submit to the Word of God, and laid hands on his uncovered eyes. I then prayed with all my heart.

After removing my hands, I stepped back ten feet or so, whipped out my phone and asked him to again read what I'd typed. To our astonishment, he read every word flawlessly! To be certain, I typed a new set of words and stepped one to two feet further back. Again, the boy aced our little exam.

> *God also testifying with them, both by signs and wonders and by various miracles and by gifts of the Holy Spirit according to His own will* **(Hebrews 2:4).**

Now well past time I'd set aside for this chapel service, I needed to call Dillards to inform them I'd be a few minutes late for work. As swiftly as possible, I told the children goodbye, thanked the teachers, and began my short commute. I could barely contain myself. How would I get through an entire shift after just witnessing over 20 children miraculously healed in front of my face? Still, duty called. I needed to be faithful.

I pulled up to the mall, briskly slid my suit jacket on, and clocked in. Walking through the store to my department, it dawned on me that I might have time to share this story with some of my coworkers. I only had two or three more shifts to make an impact before my last day. *May as well go out with Jesus on my lips,* I thought. I took my place behind the register, and as if invisibly dragged by the sovereign hand of God, Bill approached me.

"How are you today, Josh?"

This was it. This was the opportunity I'd been waiting for. I boldly opened my mouth and began to speak. "Hey, Bill, since you asked..." I started. I didn't give him a second's hesitation to walk away. Like a runner hot off the blocks at the sound of the gun, I sprinted into the story, retelling as many of the detailed miracles I'd just witnessed in the lives and bodies of those school children.

I wasn't sure how Bill would respond, but after a few moments, I paused and waited for him to take his turn. Would he berate me? Would he walk off scoffing? Would he call the manager and attempt to have me fired?

None of the above happened! Instead, for the first time, Bill seemed to take off his jaded armor. Tears filled his eyes. His voice trembled as he looked at me with sincerity and said, "That truly touched me. Thank you for sharing it."

I was in awe. I realized in that moment that perhaps I'd just witnessed the greatest miracle of the day! The retelling of God touching those children had unlocked something in Bill's heart. He was never the same toward me after that moment. Those last few shifts were the most peaceful I'd ever experienced, as he softened his tone and even asked me further questions about my ministry.

The last hour of my last day at Dillard's, I pulled Bill and Theresa aside into the hallway of the dressing rooms. I asked Theresa to briefly share her healing testimony with Bill. She did so and he listened intently. I then spoke candidly, "Bill, to be honest, I've been afraid to talk to you about Jesus since I got here. I didn't want you to categorize me as another self-righteous jerk. The truth is, though, I'm leaving in a few hours and would be remiss if I didn't share the true gospel with you. I don't know what exactly you grew up in, or if someone hurt you in the church, but Jesus isn't like that, Bill."

For the next three to four minutes, I did my utmost to adequately share the gospel of grace. I did not exclude the need for repentance, but I sensed the Lord wanted to emphasize His love and mercy. The Lord was madly in love with Bill, and while he didn't pray with me to receive Christ in that moment, he smiled and thanked me for being an example of "a godly minister." I knew I'd done my job. I sowed my seeds. Jesus had worked with me by confirming the words I'd preached in that place with many signs following.

Since those days, I have been privileged to see God demonstrate His power to many on city streets. Sometimes, God heals the grocery store clerk. Other times, He gives me prophetic words to share with taxi drivers. I make a practice to tip waitresses, smile, and show kindness to gas station attendants. Still other times, I just tell people that they're amazing and that Christ loves them. I've seen many salvations through these experiences with people both inside and outside the walls of the church. People everywhere need Jesus, and it is a high honor to be invited into the process of leading them to His redemptive arms.

God did not ordain angels to preach the gospel. For whatever reason, He chose us—His church. We may be finite people, sometimes limited by our own fleshly circumstances, but God promises that if we will seek to love as He did, He will work alongside us in bringing many to reconciliation. What a privilege to co-labor *with* the King, still living and active here on the earth!

Pandemic Evangelism

In the year of the deadly COVID pandemic, my life was altered not merely by the societal effects everyone was experiencing, but in personal ways as well. In the spring of that year, I was in a freak car accident. Thankfully no one was injured, but I was taken to the hospital for observation overnight. They ran cautionary tests, but everything came back negative. I was released the next day and went about my business.

A few weeks later, though, I received a letter from the Secretary of State's office. To my shock, the letter claimed they believed me to be a danger to the road. Therefore, I would need to surrender my license immediately. What?! After 20-plus years of a near spotless driving record, I couldn't fathom why the state would suddenly deem me a threat to the roadways. Nevertheless, they did, and I had no choice but to comply! Later, I discovered that one of the doctors at my local hospital had filed a paper incorrectly after my car wreck. In that document, he cited cause for concern with me behind the wheel. The state of Illinois received that letter and followed through.

It's a strange feeling going from free access to transportation to suddenly having none whatsoever. This was especially true in a rural community. There were no subways or taxis in my part of the state. So, in the spring of 2020, with a pandemic already limiting travel and human interaction, I was forced into greater solitary confinement. To make matters worse, my car battery stopped working the same week. So, even in case of an emergency, I was unable to drive!

Though this was discouraging, I went into my room, shut the door, and fell to my knees. "Lord, I know it's not the end of the world, but this is a rather shocking turn of events. My home feels as though it has suddenly become a prison all over again. But I choose to praise You! Thank You for giving me a home and thank You for using this time for Your glory. I also pray You pay the devil back for any involvement he may have in this!"

A few days later, I received a text from a trusted prophetic friend, Aaron Yarnall, who lived in Nashville, Tennessee. He said he felt led to ask if I'd ever considered putting a few of our ministry's videos on TikTok. At first, I was revolted by the idea. From what I'd understood, TikTok was an app mainly filled with teenagers obnoxiously lip syncing and dancing to 60 second song clips. Aaron was adamant, however, as it was a virtually unworked harvest field for Christ.

The following day, another trusted prophetic friend, Jon-Mark Baker, called me on the phone. Unaware of the text I'd received the previous day from Aaron, JonMark said he felt led to ask if I'd ever considered posting ministry videos on TikTok! This seemed far too coincidental, so I thanked him for reaching out and decided to give it a shot.

TikTok Harvest

That night, I downloaded TikTok's app, opened an account and edited four or five videos to post. One video contained a clip of Zach Rutledge (one of our young adults at Loft Church) praying for a high school girl's leg to supernaturally grow out. She'd had chronic pain for years in her hip, but by the end of the 60-second clip, the girl was screaming and weeping in shock. She had tangibly felt her hips and legs shift during prayer, and when she stood up, all the pain was gone.

I posted this clip and a few others before falling asleep. When I woke up, I expected the videos to have received maybe a few hundred views. When I clicked on my account, however, I was stunned to see Zach's video had already been seen by almost a quarter of a million people! Five hours later, that number hit one million. By the next day, the video had been seen over 2.3 million times!

Suddenly, my inbox was flooded with messages from teenagers all around the world. Many were very broken, describing situations of physical, emotional, and sexual abuse. Others were cutting themselves, depressed, or suicidal. Still others just came straight out and asked, "I want to know Jesus. How can I be saved?" Overwhelmed by the gravity of these messages, I wept. I was deeply moved by how candid these children were. There was no pretense, no façade as so often is the case with adults. These young souls were so desperately crying out for rescue, they were willing to trust a complete stranger with the most intimate details of their life if even a glimmer of hope might result.

After praying for wisdom, I made a few calls and recruited young adults from our church community to form a social media team. We funneled communication from TikTok through our church's Instagram account and everyone went to work responding to needs. We also livestreamed several times from our account.

Through this interaction, we were able to lead a few hundred children to salvation in Christ in less than four weeks. Not wanting to have the new converts immediately left to fend for themselves, I produced a series of discipleship videos on our website to aid in their growth. In addition, we saw countless miraculous healings and teens being filled with the

Spirit. Some were healed as our team sent audible prayers through Instagram. Others were touched via livestreaming. The ease in which the Holy Spirit seemed to reveal Himself to these teenagers moved us all. With sometimes just a word, broken bones, migraines, stomach conditions, or lumps on their bodies were healed instantly. Most of these teenagers had no grid for anything in Jesus!

When praying for the Holy Spirit to fall over live broadcasts, we gave them no descriptions of what they might experience. After a few seconds of delay, one teenager after another would say things like, "Oh my God, I feel heat all over my body," or "I'm crying so hard, it felt like God just hugged me." Others said, "My mouth is quivering, and I can't stop making these sounds, words I don't understand!" Months later, when the numbers of TikTok viewers finally began to wane, I stood back in awe of what the Lord had brought about.

The gospel is always a green light, but He can bear so much more fruit through us if we learn to follow His lead. This is the difference between working for Him and working *with* Him. Our invitation to co-labor with heaven is always being offered. To get God's results, we must learn to submit to God's leadings.

Pakistan Harvest

Within just a few weeks of the heavenly harvest I experienced through TikTok, I received an invitation from a pastor and evangelist in Pakistan to minister to a remote village through

Zoom. In addition, this pastor owned a large satellite network in Lahore and wanted to know if I'd be interested in hosting a show.

To be honest, I likely would not have accepted this invitation if not for a prophetic word I'd received two years earlier. During a trip in 2018 to Northern California, I was introduced to a woman over coffee who many deemed a true, new covenant prophet. Her name was Cindy Sauvain. French by birth, Cindy spoke fast and with a thick accent. After a brief introduction, she began to share with me what she prophetically sensed from the Lord. To this day, I have rarely received words more astoundingly accurate. She not only precisely described my personality and character, but also disparaging words people had spoken in my past to unjustly malign me—and how God was going to redeem those situations.

Cindy also told me about a manual I would write for a ministry within Loft Church, and that it would be used to set many free. What she didn't know was I was literally in the process of writing that manual. It was for development of an inner-healing and deliverance ministry within our church.

Finally, Cindy said, "Oh, and I see Pakistan over you. God is going to open a large door there for you to minister." Up until that moment, I had been tracking with her. When she said "Pakistan," though, I thought to myself, *I'm a white boy from the middle of nowhere in the Midwest. I don't know anyone in Pakistan, nor am I sure they'd want to know me!*

Two years later, when I received a significant invitation to minister in Pakistan, I remembered Cindy's word. What was God up to? I decided to step out in faith. Not long after, I ministered to that remote village through Zoom. These were a people literally "in the dirt." In fact, although the evangelism team owned a projector, the village had no television or screen to view. My image was instead being projected upon a large, white sheet. I was greatly moved they were humble enough to allow a young man from America to talk to them in this way.

Now, Pakistan is predominately a Muslim nation, so when it came time to give an invitation to receive Christ, I assumed only a few people would raise their hands in response. To my surprise, over 90 percent of the village waved their arms exuberantly to repent of their sins and surrender to the Lordship of Jesus Christ! When I prayed for healing, many also raised their hands to report external issues—that could be immediately tested—had vanished. Jesus was so faithful! The moment the broadcast ended, I wept profusely behind my desk. I couldn't get over the humility of these people, or that God would entrust me with their hearts.

Over the next few months, I also hosted several broadcasts over Pastor John's television network. Over the course of that time, hundreds of thousands viewed our program, and approximately one thousand people received Jesus as Lord. During the fall and winter months of 2020, I was invited to do several crusades in Pakistan with crowds of nearly 5,000 people. In each meeting we held, thousands gave their lives to Jesus.

After our last crusade in December, I pondered all that had taken place during the year. In a time of global pandemic, when few live evangelism events would be possible—in a year when the state of Illinois had revoked my driver's license confining me to home—I had seen more people saved than in my whole life! That year, I was privileged to personally lead over 10,000 souls to Jesus. All of this occurred from my home office while wearing track pants. I couldn't go to the nations, so the Lord brought the nations to me!

> *Now I want you to know, brethren, that my circumstances have turned out for the greater progress of the gospel* **(Philippians 1:12).**

The church must continue taking the spiritual kingdom by force. The time for religious little prayer gatherings is over. We can't pray angels into preaching the gospel. I'm not saying prayer isn't part of the kingdom, but it's time we also get in the game. We must give ourselves fully to Christ's commission. A move of God happens when people of God move. The kingdom of heaven is near, and I don't mean a rapture. I mean the church living out loud in a world needing salvation.

> *Behold, I say to you, lift up your eyes and look on the fields, that they are white for harvest* **(John 4:35).**

CHAPTER 13

SUFFERING WITH GOD

These trials will show that your faith is genuine. It is being tested as fire tests and purifies gold—though your faith is far more precious than mere gold **(1 Peter 1:7 NLT).**

A few years ago, a young man in his 20s wrote to me. Only a few sentences into his letter, and a tone of frustration was already seeping through the pages. He seemed under the impression I'd been handed a supernatural silver spoon at birth. My life had been seasoned with untrammeled blessing, while his own was found immutably wanting.

"You know, it's not fair," he scathingly wrote. "You have this church where all of these miracles happen. You've had it easy while my life has been filled with hardship!"

Perhaps in reading this book thus far, you've had similar thoughts. Perhaps you've concluded I'm suggesting if you'll just get your spiritual ducks in order, you'll fall headlong into supernatural dialogue, miracles, and blessing. Is that what I'm suggesting? Yes and no.

While I believe the biblical principles I've laid out thus far will enable you to better engage the kingdom of heaven on earth, I'd be disingenuous to suggest the journey is not without peril. The truth is, while principles and proper doctrine are always of merit, our journeys also require seasons of preparation, character building, and yes, even godly suffering. It is this bifurcation of truth that fashions our path to His Presence.

> *That I may know Him and the power of His resurrection and the fellowship of His sufferings, being conformed to His death; in order that I may attain to the resurrection from the dead* **(Philippians 3:10-11).**

It may be surprising to read a so-called charismatic author talking about suffering. But I will not sweep the uncomfortable parts of this journey under the rug. Hardship *is* part of the equation. Only, as with all things in God, the reality must not be overgeneralized. Instead, suffering must be put in proper perspective—in its right place against the broader new covenant framework.

> *Be diligent to present yourself approved to God... rightly dividing the word of truth* **(2 Timothy 2:15 NKJV).**

Rather than answer the young man's letter in writing, it seemed more appropriate to give him a phone call. He was desiring to one day be in full-time ministry, and I wanted to ensure he had a better grasp of what may be required. Hardship is universal, after all. We may experience different versions, but it's helpful to hear about the weak moments in a life as well as the strong. It reminds us we all need God's grace!

When the man answered his phone, I said, "Received your note, brother. I think there are some things you need to better understand about my journey. If you really want to know how I got to my present season in God, I'll tell you, but it will take a few minutes."

He agreed to listen carefully. In order correct some of his assumptions, I would need to take him back to the very beginning of my story—my literal birth.

I Should Not Have Been Born

The devil has tried to kill me many times, including while in my mother's womb. My parents had three children before me, but the third, Andrew, only survived for a few hours after his birth. Shortly after his death, the doctors discovered a rare blood disorder. The condition, they said, was degenerative and gave little hope to my parents for subsequent children. In fact, the physicians strongly advised against it.

At that time, my parents were believers in Christ, but they hadn't yet learned much about healing or the power of the Holy Spirit. Because the loss of Andrew was excruciatingly painful, they attempted to take the doctors' advice to avoid another tragedy.That is, until nine years later when my mother suddenly discovered she was pregnant during a ministry trip to Holland. After returning home, she reported to the doctor's office for a round of preliminary testing. Receiving back the results, the doctor sat both of my parents down to deliver sobering news:

"I'm sorry to inform you, Mr. and Mrs. Adkins, that this child's condition is as we expected. The blood counts are off in such a way, he appears to have the same condition as his brother."

My parents' hearts sank as the physicians continued, "We want to prepare you for the worst. This child will likely not survive the pregnancy. If it does, it will be in a vegetative state for life. You should know that abortion is also a viable option."

Doing their best to brave the bad news, my father and mother returned home to consider the doctors' reports. However, by this point in their life, they had grown in the knowledge of Christ's supernatural power. So, they quickly came to a firm decision. They would contend for my perfect health by standing on the Word of God and prayer. Specifically, my mother declared one psalm over me every single day. She would lay hands on her belly and recite:

> *I shall not die, but live, and declare the works of the Lord* **(Psalm 118:17 NKJV).**

One month later, Mom returned to the hospital for a checkup. The doctors ran tests, but the results were as before. Nothing had changed. She would not give up that easily, though. My mom returned home, praised God for my healing, declared the Scripture over my life, then returned to the doctors the following month. The same tests were run, but with the same results. This pattern repeated for over six months. Blood counts remained far outside of their normal range. However, in the seventh month of my mother's pregnancy, something happened. This time, after testing, the blood counts all came back perfectly normal. The doctors couldn't explain it. All they said was, "We don't know how this happened, but it looks like you may have this baby after all."

My mother knew exactly how it had happened. Encouraged by what she believed was a miracle taking place, Mom made another request of God. She said to my father, "Mike, all three of my babies have gotten progressively bigger. Andrew was a difficult labor. I really don't want to go through that again if I don't have to. Agree with me in prayer that this child won't exceed eight pounds." My father agreed.

On March 1, 1982, in the wee hours of the morning, my mother went into labor. When I arrived, I was not only completely healthy, but I weighed exactly 8.0 pounds on the nose! This was precisely my mother's prayer! God answered to the ounce, and I still have the birth certificate to prove it! I am beyond grateful to Jesus and my parents for believing His promises. Satan tried to snuff me out, but his power was inferior to that of God's Word and Spirit.

Now, I'm not saying I'm someone special. Satan seems to desire to steal, kill, and destroy all believers. Still, the Scripture is clear that although he's not omniscient, the devil can to some degree know the future (see Acts 16:23). Perhaps he had caught wind of God's sovereign call upon my life. Regardless, here I am, committed to destroying the devil's kingdom with all I am in Christ. This is my life-offering back to God, for He rescued me from the lion's den (see 1 Pet. 5:8)!

Something in the Water

When I was six years old, my father planned a visit to an old childhood friend. This man had a nice house in the country, with a farm pond stocked with fish. Knowing that I particularly liked fishing at the time, my father decided to take me along. After arriving, we talked for a while with the man and his wife inside their house before being invited to take their boat out on the pond.

I remember it was a chilly, late November day. We were dressed in flannels, jeans, and boots to keep warm. When dad and I climbed in the boat, we noticed one life jacket lying in a small puddle of water near the bow. Not wanting to get my clothes dirty, I asked if I could go without the vest. My father complied, likely thinking the pond was small enough a life vest wasn't warranted. Besides, our boat was quaint enough to need only an electric trolling motor and paddles. So, how dangerous could the situation really be?

We pushed off from shore. Dad and I sat on opposite ends of the boat, while the trolling motor's gentle propulsion seemed to "hum" us into deeper waters. My attention span held for a few seconds, before that six-year-old need for further stimulation kicked in. That's when I spotted an electronic fish finder on my father's end of the boat. Fascinated, I asked, "Dad, can I come see the fish?" He smiled and waved me over. I stood up and began walking toward the center. Suddenly, the weight of the cheaply made boat shifted dramatically. My father's weightier end dipped just enough below the surface of the pond to allow a cascade of water to come pouring in. No more than five seconds later and the entire vessel had disappeared beneath the surface and my father and I with it! My father had lunged for me, but he was too late. Gravity had pulled me out of reach.

The trouble was, at six years old I hadn't yet learned to swim. Compounding the problem, the winter coat and boots meant to remedy November's cold temperatures now had become a greater danger. I sank like a rock. While instinctively holding my breath, I remember looking up and seeing the glimmer of sunlight from the surface quickly fading. A murky darkness enveloped my senses. I was going to drown.

Suddenly, I felt what I can only describe as two hands grabbing my ankles and moving them in a rhythmic kicking motion while simultaneously pushing me upward. It was as if I suddenly had fins! Within seconds, I surfaced. This time, my father grabbed hold of my arm, put me on his shoulders, and began to swim.

In a moment when a child who couldn't swim ought to be panicked, I instead had an irrational peace. Rather than screaming and crying in fear, I calmly said, "Help us, Jesus." To this day, I don't know how I had the wisdom to pray that, except by the Holy Spirit.

A few moments later, my dad's toes touched the underwater bank of the shoreline. We crawled onto the tiny beach and collapsed to catch our breath. My father was especially gasping, coughing, and spitting up water. Later he told me that he was seconds away from drowning himself. The weight of my body on his shoulders had caused his mouth to fall just below the surface, and he was taking water into his lungs.

We almost died. But God!

Now, unlike my birth story, I'm not sure I can lay the full blame for this accident on satan. Perhaps the devil is into manufacturing poor quality fishing boats. That's debatable! Regardless, what I do know is that Jesus answered my cry. He truly saved our lives, and I will go to my grave believing those two hands that grabbed my ankles belonged to a guardian angel.

My purpose in relaying these near-death experiences is to say that although God has sent His Holy Spirit to facilitate a kingdom of heaven upon the earth, that doesn't mean we won't face opposition in this life. No, even Spirit-filled, tongue-talking Christians will face various trials and tribulations. Some are authored by the devil himself, designed to snuff out the lives of saints called to fulfill God's purposes in the earth.

> *I have told you these things, so that in me you may have peace. In this world you will have trouble. But take heart! I have overcome the world* **(John 16:33 NIV).**

Pathway to Purpose

Not all opposition we face in this life is the product of satan. Some is of our own doing. Other hardships are actually used by God!

> *Through whom also we have obtained our introduction by faith into this grace in which we stand; and we exult in hope of the glory of God. And not only this, but we also exult in our tribulations, knowing that tribulation brings about perseverance; and perseverance, proven character; and proven character, hope; and hope does not disappoint* **(Romans 5:2-5).**

Many leaders in the Scripture underwent processes of conditioning and character refinement credited to God Himself. Joseph was thrown in prison. Israel was placed in a desert. David hid in caves. Even Jesus spent 40 days in the wilderness. Satan didn't lead Him there. The Bible says the Holy Spirit did!

> *Then Jesus was led up by the Spirit into the wilderness to be tempted by the devil* **(Matthew 4:1).**

Unfortunately, I did not recognize this reality until several years into God's processes in my own life. The Lord had deposited the call, but I also lacked wisdom. I thought that since He had given me a measure of the Spirit's anointing and power, I deserved to immediately be thrust into the

Reinhard Bonnke evangelism crusade fields. Either that, or the fact I had earned an undergrad degree entitled me to a high-paying job until Reinhard called! I know—a real face-palm mindset.

In the meantime, I made a costly mistake. In a flood of rushed emotion, I got engaged to a girl I met in college. We moved to Knoxville, Tennessee in search of a new life together. She was a beautiful person, but in hindsight, we jumped into the engagement prematurely. It fell apart nine months later. My fiancée was hurt. Our families and friends were hurt. I felt outrageous levels of confusion and guilt. Most of our mutual acquaintances broke off all contact. I lost a lot of friends.

At night, I would lie in bed riddled with a level of shame I'd never experienced. To say I wept would be an understatement. For months, I cudgeled myself for the pain I'd caused so many people—chiefly, my fiancée. I thought if I hated myself enough, some of those I'd inadvertently hurt might somehow sense how sorry I was and have mercy. It didn't work. Instead, the hatred I inflicted upon myself not only harmed my intangible parts, but it began affecting my body as well.

One day, a bizarre incident occurred during my lunch break at work. I was eating Chinese takeout, when suddenly the food I'd swallowed got stuck in my esophagus. The only way to clear my throat was to throw up on the front lawn of my workplace. It was embarrassing, but the moment passed, so I wrote it off as a fluke. Unfortunately, this incident was merely a preview of worse things to come.

In need of a fresh start, I returned to my hometown in southern Illinois. With little savings, I found a government-subsidized housing apartment near our local park. Though I was thankful for that little place, it felt as though my life's purpose had been inevitably suspended. Not only did I have no family. Now I had no job, let alone direction. I was home, but I felt as much in a wilderness as ever. In an attempt to help, my father hired me to ship packages from his home office.

One day, we had a terrific storm that knocked down hundreds of trees in the woods of my parents' property. Seeing this as an opportunity for more available work for his son, my father asked me to pick up fallen branches in his woods. He'd pay me $40 for a few hours of outdoor labor each day. It was a job. I was grateful. Still, I thought to myself, *The guy who believed he would be immediately thrust into evangelistic crusades is now literally picking up sticks for a living! What a success!*

This humbling situation lasted for three years. I tried not to complain, but more than a few times I offered it to God. "This all seems so meaningless! How low do I have to go before You allow me a ministry, Lord?" I had no idea the greatest test of my life was yet to come.

Hell on Earth

One day, before starting my daily shift in the woods, I ate lunch with my family. There was nothing especially unusual about that day, or the meal we had. Five minutes after eating, though, I noticed another uncomfortable feeling in my esophagus. This time, food remained stuck. I could neither swallow it fully nor throw it up. I walked around the dining room table, pushing downward upon my breastbone with my hand. I tried drinking water. That only made matters worse. Then, I went outside to see if the fresh air might help. The food simply would not budge. The pain in my chest had now become unbearable, and I felt lightheaded. Finally, I said to my father, "Something is wrong." That was the last thing I remember.

I passed out in the yard for several minutes while my father stood over me praying and trying to bring me to. When I finally regained consciousness, I was so weak I needed assistance walking. For the first time in my life, I was rushed to the emergency room. Our local physicians did the best they could to assess my situation, but the only plausible reason they could give for this episode was a muscle spasm. They told me it was likely a fluke incident and sent me home.

They couldn't have been more wrong.

A few months later, I was out to eat with some friends when I had another food impaction. This time, though, not only did food get stuck in my esophagus, but I had an anaphylactic reaction. My lungs tightened as I fought to squeeze air through the suddenly inflamed passages. After 20 minutes of agonizing shortness of breath, my lungs slowly opened. However, my body trembled for hours afterward, likely from both the physical shock and unknown cause of these worsening episodes.

Over the next three months, I was rushed to our local emergency room ten times. The food impaction had now become a lesser of two evils. I would more often have long bouts of shortness of breath while feeling poisoned. Since these episodes seemed to be worse after meals, I had increasing difficulty eating enough to be adequately nourished. After a few of those emergency visits, I was admitted to our local hospital, but no one could find a physiological cause for my issues. Doctors began suggesting vague "catch-alls" like anxiety or depression. But my family and friends knew me well enough to know this wasn't merely in my head. Other than an occasional cold or stomach bug, I'd never been sick a day in my life. Now, I was fighting for air daily while reaching a dangerously low body weight. I lost nearly 30 pounds and was eventually bedridden.

Finally, my sister Tricia (a registered nurse) was able to have me transferred to a larger hospital in St. Louis, Missouri. In doing so, she saved my life. Had I gone a few more weeks in the condition I was in, I would have died. While in St. Louis, I saw over 30 physicians in nearly every department. Some were world-renowned specialists in their field, yet after a week, we still had no answers!

One afternoon, I gathered enough strength to slowly walk my frail body from the hospital bed to a window. My room overlooked one of the city's most beautiful attractions, Forrest Park. I stood watching the people below. Some were walking or running on trails. Others picnicked as couples or with their families. There was so much life. Health seemed the last of their concerns, yet in the prime years of my young life, I was squarely looking at the possibility of death.

At that moment, I made an internal decision. I had virtually no physical strength. My mind was exhausted. My emotional state dripped with despair. Yet deep inside, in a place beyond all those natural senses, existed an unwavering faith in the God of my youth. With stammered breath, I said to the Lord, "I refuse to die until Your will for my life is complete. I trust You. I trust You." There was no electrifying excitement in the room. No "amens" were offered by a crowd. All I had was Christ in me.

The last doctor I was scheduled to see (a gastroenterologist) performed an endoscopy of my esophagus. There he found the first hard evidence of a problem. A massive amount of white blood cells had gone rogue and collected in my throat. It was a rare condition called "eosinophilic esophagitis." Say that three times fast!

The doctor explained in layman's terms that when I'd eat, my immune system would attack both the food and my own esophagus. This would cause my throat and lung tissue to swell in a way akin to asthma. The only known treatment for this condition at the time was an oral steroid to coat the esophageal lining. They gave it to me immediately, and thankfully I saw some improvement—enough to be discharged anyway.

I was alive, but extremely frail. At 5 feet 11 inches, I now weighed a meager 124 pounds. Being in no condition to live alone, I was forced to move in with my parents. I want to say on record: I am forever grateful to my family for taking me in. Though I was embarrassed to be in this situation as a 29-year-old man, my mother and father were extremely compassionate and generous. My mother cooked for me, while my father made endless calls and trips to doctors and pharmacies.

It actually took years to fully unpack what was happening inside my body. We knew the basics of the general condition, but no one at that time, including my doctors, realized that my immune system had produced antibodies for nearly every type of food I'd ingested before being hospitalized. We discovered later that I was allergic to over 40 foods! In addition, we didn't know the condition also existed within my intestines. That meant sometimes being sick up to 36 hours after ingesting a food my body disagreed with. When I made an error with my food choices, I would sometimes have episodes of passing out, or at least trembling with the feeling of being poisoned for up to five to six hours at a time. I did my best to gain weight and strength, but it was an uphill battle.

Traveling at this time also became torturous. I couldn't be in an automobile longer than 10 minutes without suffering tremendously, as apparently I'd developed an allergy to dust mites as well. For this reason, I was rarely able to leave my parents' home. I lived this kind of personal hell for three years, never knowing which brand of physical torture lurked beyond the next hour.

At one point, my father stuck a post-it note to a flower vase sitting near the chair in which I most often sat. He'd written in black felt marker, "Don't doubt God's love for you!" Hundreds of times, I sat staring at that note while trembling with weakness and shortness of breath. Hundreds of times, I screamed from within, "Where are You, God? What have I done wrong? Do You really love me?"

When a man or woman is thoroughly tortured, fickle façades of faith are swallowed up by pain. Hopelessness knocks loudly at his or her door. I would be lying if I said I'd not many times been tempted to answer. My faith in God was greatly tested.

By the end of my second year of being ill, I realized the full weight of my situation. I was 31 years old. I had no family, no ministry, no job, no savings, and I lived with my parents. My body looked more like that of a teenage boy than a grown man. Nearly everything I knew of freedom or pleasure had been stripped from me. Still, something inside refused to quit. My flesh and soul may at times have doubted, but my spirit knew too much—it knew Jesus was still on the throne. His Word and the miracles I'd experienced could not be erased from my heart.

> *So Jesus said to the twelve, "You do not want to go away also, do you?" Simon Peter answered Him, "Lord, to whom shall we go? You have words of eternal life"* **(John 6:67-68).**

Lessons Learned

Many times, in that season I read and took comfort in the story of Joseph. He had been given enormous dreams as a young man, only to find himself thrown into an ancient prison where he remained for nearly a decade! What testing he must have endured! How often did he cry out in despair to God? Yet Joseph did not let go of the promise, and God was faithful to fulfill it.

Likewise, David was anointed the chosen king of God's nation as a boy. Yet he underwent over a decade of trial and wilderness before taking his throne. How much character developed in those caves? How much of David's youthful flesh did God need to strip before he could sustain a kingship without corruption? Yet David endured. The crown he was promised as a child only fit properly after he'd become a man.

What about Jesus? How difficult was it for the Son of God to deny Himself a miraculous escape from temptations faced in the wilderness, let alone the cross? What kind of humility did it take for the heavenly Messiah to submit to such earthly processes?

> *Although He was a Son, He learned obedience from the things which He suffered. And having been made perfect, He became to all those who obey Him the source of eternal salvation* **(Hebrews 5:8-9).**

Now, I know without a doubt that God did not directly cause my sickness. Sometimes we suffer demonic attacks. Other times, we endure consequences of our thoughts and actions. Demons can even take advantage of our ignorance, only compounding the issue. Nevertheless, despite many fervent prayers for healing and deliverance, God did not immediately rescue me from this trial. This one, I had to walk through. I had to learn to wait *with* Him in the suffering. I'm not saying there wasn't a potential key to my "breakthrough." I'm simply saying, despite many years of exhausting efforts to find it, I didn't.

In hindsight, I saw the hand of God at work in my life. The long, arduous heat of that desert season wilted much of my flesh. Selfish ambition starved. Entitlements withered. Pride in who I was, what I had, or even what I looked like burned away in the purging fires of suffering. Instead, I better understood pain. Consequently, compassion for those with illness (no matter the type) now flooded my heart. I could also relate to those with feelings of hopelessness and despair. Beyond all of this, I learned the art of perseverance—to believe and find contentment in the invisible God even when all that is visible crumbles around me.

I've heard people say, "When you find your passions, you find who you are." Perhaps, but the word *passion* means "to suffer." So, the reality is, we are what we're willing to suffer for. When we no longer live for ourselves, we are as Christ.

> *I have been crucified with Christ and I no longer live, but Christ lives in me. The life I now live in the body, I live by faith in the Son of God, who loved me and gave himself for me* **(Galatians 2:20 NIV).**

I can truly say, most everything good and of lasting significance in my life has come by way of death and resurrection. If a gift, dream, or desire has been of consequence, God has often asked me to first nail it to the cross. I've had to bury it and wait for Him alone to roll away the stone. This process has afforded me little opportunity for self-promotion or self-sustainment. Instead, I have known for certain when the resurrection of that thing has taken place, it was only by the faithfulness of God.

Until the fire God puts inside us can be fully breathed out, it must pass through our inward parts, finishing its assigned work before reaching exhale. From such processes of ordained waiting, we gain the character and God gets the glory. When He both authors and publishes our dreams, they become legacy, bearing fruit not only in our lifetime, but for generations to come.

> *They afflicted his feet with fetters, he himself was laid in irons; until the time that his word came to pass, the word of the Lord tested him* **(Psalm 105:18-19).**

Crossing Over

After explaining these events and life lessons to my young friend on the phone (you thought I'd forgotten about him, didn't you?), there was a long moment of silence before he responded. It was a lot to take in, but in his next words he conveyed a sense of gratitude for sharing my sufferings. He even apologized for his brashness in presuming his trials had outweighed my own.

I finished our conversation by telling him the good news of it all. After just over three years in the nightmare of sickness and confinement in my parents' house, I suddenly took a positive turn. I wasn't fully healed, but my body began processing food better than it had since the sickness began. I put on weight and gained strength. Consequently, I was able to leave the house more often and drive further than before. At that same time, the Lord opened a door for a well-paying job. This one didn't require strenuous physical labor, so I was able to fulfill its duties without issue. That employment allowed me to finally move out of my parents' house and into that *loft* apartment you've already read much about. This was my pathway to fuller measures of His Presence, including the first phases of full-time ministry.

Now, I'm not suggesting everyone needs to face these same trials in their life. I'm also not saying everyone must endure the same intensity or time of suffering I did. Hopefully, for most, it will be less. For others, it might be more. Either way, the principles of preparation, testing, and character development hold true for all people in Christ. Want to become something great? God must make you small first.

> *Consider it all joy, my brethren, when you encounter various trials, knowing that the testing of your faith produces endurance. And let endurance have its perfect result, so that you may be perfect and complete, lacking in nothing* **(James 1:2-3).**

As I've noted, some trials do come at the doing of the devil. Others may be consequences of our own poor actions. Still others may be part of God's refining fire. I can point to all three elements sometimes simultaneously existing in my journey. Regardless, hardships come to all. When they do, we must be prepared to cling to the Savior. Nothing else but the

Person of Jesus can sustain us in the hellfires of this life. But He *is* enough! If He doesn't immediately rescue us, He will be the fourth man in the flame (see Dan. 3:24-26).

Discerning God, Bad, and Ugly

I'd be remiss if I ended a section on suffering without attempting to offer a general guidepost for distinguishing between the different sources of it. After all, the Bible says that we are to judge one kind, resist another, and embrace with perseverance the other still. Therefore, we cannot take the easy route of overgeneralization. No, suffering must be rightly divided. So, how do we do so?

Mistakes and Mayhem

Before we distinguish God's actions from the devil's, let's deal with our own issues first!

Not everything is satan's fault. I'm not offering him sympathy in saying that, but just stating a fact. Warfare is real, but some Christians are naïve to think *everything* is the devil. Not only is it naïve, but detrimental to believe we can forgo our own responsibilities in choosing righteousness just because satan exists. The devil doesn't make us do everything, nor does he cause every negative circumstance in our life. People have free will. We can make our own mistakes. Others can act imperfectly against us. Everyone is in process. This is why Jesus spoke so regularly on humility and forgiveness! These are vital to uncap the balm of healing.

> *Therefore, confess your sins to one another, and pray for one another so that you may be healed* **(James 5:16).**

Sometimes, in the ethos of millions making spontaneous free choices, accidents just happen! Not every car wreck resulting from running a red light is some sinister spiritual plot against us. Nor is it always someone's desire to harm. There are over seven billion on the planet and a bit of chaos obviously at work in a groaning earth. Sometimes, we're just living life in a crowded room! Other times, we are our own worst enemy.

> *But each one is tempted when he is carried away and enticed by his own lust. Then when lust has conceived, it gives birth to sin; and when sin is accomplished, it brings forth death* **(James 1:14-15).**

When we encounter a trial, it is wise to initially look inward. Paul said we ought to judge ourselves first (see 1 Cor. 11:31). Therefore, it is important to take some time to ask the Lord if a difficult circumstance is a consequence of our own sin. If so, the Holy Spirit will be faithful to reveal it. Then, we may simply approach His merciful throne in repentance and receive grace for our need (see Heb. 4:16). However, sometimes natural consequences need a little time to run their course. If a conflict involves another free-will human being especially, relief may not be immediate. In such a case, we can ask for grace to help us walk steadily until we've seen the hardship fully through.

That said, believers can make the mistake of digging their own grave of guilt even if there has been no evidence of a crime. Though humility and self-examination are noble to a degree, to weary oneself through excessive introspection is dangerous. If we've sought the Lord for our own lustful causes of consequence and come up empty, or if our ideas of judgment are misaligned with the Word of God, we only do further damage to ourselves in the midst of a trial. False accusation can be just as damaging to ourselves as it can be against others. Demons also love to capitalize on such things.

Therefore, I always counsel to only initially examine oneself honestly before the Lord. If after a short time of seeking nothing is revealed, then it is time to do as Paul instructed:

> *And having done everything* [you know], *to stand firm. Stand firm therefore, having girded your loins with truth, and having put on the breastplate of righteousness* **(Ephesians 6:13-14).**

Satan from Sovereignty

Now the obvious remaining question is, then, if not from mere individual sin, how do we know if a source of suffering is from God or the devil? I love my friend Joshua Silverberg's answer to this question. He puts it so simply, "If it's hindering you from worshiping or fulfilling your *immediate* purposes in God, it's likely not from God."

Of course, the Bible ought to be the ultimate plumb line for determining spiritual truths, but using any old Scripture won't always do. Christ ushered in a new covenant established upon greater promises, so we must prioritize our use of Scriptures to accurately assess and respond to spiritual forces at play in our modern lives.

For example, while the book of Job is a timeless tale of suffering, it should not be our go-to source of revelation on the matter. That's not to say the book of Job can't provide insights, but Jesus' life and ministry is our most up-to-date source material for applicable revelation. That's because while noble men existed throughout the Scriptures, their knowledge was finite, and their lives were also imperfect.

Jesus, on the other hand, had access to the full knowledge of God and His will for creation. He lived perfectly, heard perfectly, and understood the sometimes-complex dynamics of spiritual authorities in play (i.e. the devil, consequences for sin, man's delegated authority, etc.). Not to mention, Jesus' mission fulfilled the law of Moses and introduced updated heavenly perspectives, principles, and powers to us!

Simply put, Jesus modeled perfect theology. He is therefore the surer way to determine the source of a hardship.

> *And He is the radiance of His glory and the exact representation of His nature and upholds all things by the word of His power* **(Hebrews 1:3).**

The life of the apostles and first church in Acts is a wonderful secondary source of proper interpretation. While men and women of theological renown argue over exegesis of Paul's letters, Acts can often aid in properly interpreting the epistles. The book of Acts is history, after all—actions revealing the meaning behind many of the epistles' words and original intent.

So, what do we find in these relevant biblical examples? Curses, sicknesses, diseases, extreme poverty, demonization—these are all largely laid at the feet of the devil's doing. The kingdom of God that Jesus demonstrated and instructed His followers to model became a remedy for these areas of brokenness. So, in this, we ought to not embrace but adamantly resist these things!

> *Submit therefore to God. Resist the devil and he will flee from you* **(James 4:7).**

If God desired us to accept all suffering as sovereign, why would He instruct us to resist the devil and his doing? Because not all suffering is sovereignly given. It may be allowed, but even an allowance does not necessarily indicate God's direct permission. We live in a battle zone. The earth is undergoing fiery trials day and night, and much of it is the devil's doing (see 2 Cor. 4:4). It's never a good idea then to blame God for that for which satan is responsible.

> *Every good thing given and every perfect gift is from above, coming down from the Father of lights, with whom there is no variation or shifting shadow* **(James 1:17).**

The crux of differentiating God's doing from the devil's doing is this: When hardship is of heaven, it is seasonal. When of the devil, hardship seeks to permanently destroy. See, the devil puts us in unpleasant circumstances for the purpose of killing us off. God puts us in unpleasant circumstances for the purpose of building us up, making us better! Just as a personal trainer pushes an exercise client to their limits to improve them, our Father sometimes does the same. He's not rooting for our failure. He's coaching and encouraging us that we can grow—run faster, lift heavier, and become stronger overall in His kingdom.

Satan is the author of some hardships. Still, grapes must be crushed to make wine. Diamonds form under pressure. Olives are pressed to make oil. Seeds must first fall to the ground before bearing much fruit. The Lord's intent is that we develop character able to embrace His fullness and sustain greater levels of His glory. Ultimately, to become like Him!

> *For you, God, tested us; you refined us like silver* **(Psalm 66:10 NIV).**

Persecution and Martyrdom

Finally, there is a suffering in the Scripture promised above all others. It is of a different type than all the rest. That is persecution. Jesus promised it would be a sign of truly following Him (see John 15:20). Paul reiterates this by saying, "All who desire to live godly in Christ Jesus will suffer persecution" (2 Tim. 3:12 NKJV).

Almost all the first 12 apostles were martyred for the gospel. Thousands more throughout church history have suffered the same fate. Think about that! Clearly, theirs wasn't a wishy-washy, drive-thru McDonald's gospel. I doubt many members of the first church communities were leaving over the paint color of the sanctuary, the type of songs played, or whether sister Martha got to bake one Sabbath instead of sister Mary. No, these people were more preoccupied with *life and death* than bickering over such petty matters as we often do today.

In the western church, we've yet to receive much physical persecution, at least to the point of shedding blood. I'm not suggesting we should wish for these things. If they happen, they happen. Still, our hearts ought to always be prepared. In the book of Revelation, Christ prophesies over seven churches. To one He says the following:

> *Do not fear what you are about to suffer. Behold, the devil is about to cast some of you into prison, so that you will be tested, and you will have tribulation for ten days. Be faithful until death, and I will give you the crown of life* **(Revelation 2:10).**

Be faithful until death?! In this instance, Jesus didn't promise anyone a *breakthrough*. He promised death. His admonishment was to be faithful regardless, knowing that on the other side of a momentary suffering would be an eternal crown of life. This is a far cry from much of the attitude of our American church especially. Yet today, many brothers and sisters around the world are being physically persecuted for their faith in Christ. Some may die before you even finish reading this chapter! What a sobering reminder of the eternal scope of our faith.

Now, I'm not suggesting that all earthly blessings are evil. It's easy to demonize receiving good in light of good people suffering. That's not God's will either. God is not against blessing. God prospers. Likewise, healing is not of the devil. Christ healed on nearly every page of the gospels for a reason. Much good we receive is for our joy and for His glory (see John 14:13; 16:24). These Christian benefits are not in contrast to the reality of persecution and even martyrdom. Again, we must rightly divide the Word of God. There is an appointed time and place for everything (see Eccles. 3:1).

Nevertheless, persecution is a vital reminder that we overcome in this life not by our blessings, but by losing our fleshly desires for God's sake. That is, in fact, how we keep heart amidst every type of suffering—whether that from which God will deliver us or that from which He won't.

> *And they overcame him by the blood of the Lamb, and by the word of their testimony; and they loved not their lives unto death* **(Revelation 12:11 KJV).**

True Christianity is not about our desires, but His. While the Bible promises some heart's desires fulfilled for those who delight in God (see Ps. 37:4), we must remember our ultimate goal is Christ Himself. If He remains our heart's utmost pursuit, we will find victory, whether in this life or the next.

For I consider that the sufferings of this present time are not worthy to be compared with the glory that is to be revealed to us **(Romans 8:18).**

Conclusions of Grandeur

We all make mistakes. We all suffer injustices. Sometimes, we will even be grown by God in uncomfortable soil. My advice is to do the best we can to differentiate sources of pain. Then, react accordingly with an inward peace. We battle better at rest. Only remember, Christlikeness is the ultimate goal, and character is becoming of leadership. So, in our faithful endurance, let us take comfort in the ever faithful One. Believe. Rightly divide the truth. Submit to God. Resist the devil, only not forgetting to exhibit character in every process. If we position our hearts correctly, we will see suffering seasons through to a harvest.

After you have suffered for a little while, the God of all grace, who called you to His eternal glory in Christ, will Himself perfect, confirm, strengthen and establish you **(1 Peter 5:10).**

However, if our suffering is one of persecution, even unto death, let us suffer nobly. For there is a life beyond this one, and as much as this book attempts to emphasize what is promised here, the glories of the hereafter far surpass the ephemeral rewards of now. Hope for the future, but ultimately hope in God Himself. Be faithful until the end.

His master said to him, "Well done, good and faithful servant" **(Mathew 25:21 AMP).**

CHAPTER 14

GLORY WITH GOD

"He was dressed in white." Those were the gleeful words of a six-year-old boy during one of our evening services at the Loft. Zane Dixon had just seen Jesus, literally standing in the center aisle of our church after a time of worship and waiting. Over the microphone, he described through a childlike lisp how Christ's clothes were so white they shone. He couldn't see Jesus' face for that light but described a purple stripe (sash) going from His shoulder down across His chest.

You might think, "What if the boy just had a vivid imagination?"

One week before this child's alleged vision, he was baptized in water. When I asked Zane in front of the entire audience why he wanted to be baptized, tears filled his eyes and his voice shook as he responded, "I love Him very much. I'm going to give my heart to Him, because He is so beautiful." Our mouths dropped. We'd never heard him talk like this. In honesty, the last few years, all we'd known from this little boy was his propensity to run around the church, punching men in the groin and occasionally putting holes in our walls. Don't get me wrong, we loved him, but he was a wild one!

Now, something was different. His heart was transformed. The fruit of behavioral change had come so rapidly, we knew it could only be God. As I pondered these events, I concluded, *Why* ***not*** *this boy? Why wouldn't Jesus choose to unveil Himself to a child?* If Scripture is true—and it is—it would seem children ought to be among the first to whom God's glory is revealed.

> *And He called a child to Himself and set him before them, and said, "Truly I say to you, unless you are converted and become like children, you will not enter the kingdom of heaven"* **(Matthew 18:2-3).**

The reality is the kingdom of God is vast. It may be veiled to some, but its depths are truly accessible to all willing to diligently seek Him (see 1 Cor. 2:10; Heb. 11:6). Only, we must come as children. That doesn't mean we can't also be cerebral. The mind is a gift and can be a powerful tool when wielded properly. But God is Spirit, and His ways are vastly superior to our natural reasonings. We must learn to submit our minds to the mind of Christ, which is known by His Spirit.

> *Which things we also speak, not in words taught by human wisdom, but in those taught by the Spirit, combining spiritual thoughts with spiritual words. But a natural* [carnally minded] *man does not accept the things of the Spirit of God,*

for they are foolishness to him; and he cannot understand them, because they are spiritually appraised **(1 Corinthians 2:13-14).**

Let us then go on to the "foolish" things!

What Is Glory?

Beyond gifts, talents, anointings, healing and deliverance miracles, there is glory. To be honest, I'm not sure most really know what glory is. It's one of those words Christians throw around vaguely, but I've rarely heard anyone thoroughly explain its nature and purpose. I have often been ignorant of its greater meanings also. In the last few years, however, God has begun illuminating depths of that word and its possibilities, especially concerning the kingdom of heaven here.

Now, I could take you through the various Hebrew and Greek terms for *glory* within the Scriptures, but it's far more expedient to simply state their most prominent meanings outright. Biblical *glory*, as defined by Strong's concordance, means "honor, renown, weight, divine quality, the [tangible] substance and/or manifestation of God's dwelling." Where in the Bible do we see the greatest depiction of these descriptors? What or Who embodies this "manifestation of God's dwelling"?

For it was the Father's good pleasure for all the fullness to dwell in Him **[Jesus] (Colossians 1:19).**

Glory is ultimately the substance of Jesus' nature. It emanates from His very being. It fills God's temple. Heaven's atmosphere swims in its fragrance. Its ether fills the air. The glory of God is in full manifestation in the third heaven always (see 2 Cor. 12:2), because there Jesus reigns supreme. Untrammeled by sin and its effects, glory floods every corner of its holy space.

So, what about the earth? Can this glory be revealed here? To what measure? Perhaps the most prominent example of glory seen upon the earth was in Jesus upon the mount of transfiguration.

> *Six days later Jesus took with Him Peter and James and John his brother, and led them up on a high mountain by themselves. And He was transfigured before them; and His face shone like the sun, and His garments became as white as light* **(Matthew 17:1-2).**

On the mountain, the glory of Jesus was revealed in the presence of three men He'd chosen. That glory manifested itself as pure light. Why light? Because that is the very nature of God.

> *God is Light, and in Him there is no darkness at all* **(1 John 1:5).**

The disciples may in times past have been dull in understanding Christ's identity, but there would be no mistaking it now—at least for Peter, James, and John. The unveiled radiance of His nature had in an instant illuminated their hearts to understand—Jesus wasn't merely a rabbi, a healer, or a friend. He was the One whom the prophet Daniel referred to as able to approach the Ancient of Days (see Dan. 7:13). He was of the same holy substance as the Father. He was God! On that mountain, the earthly tabernacle in which Jesus chose to dwell was, for a moment, swallowed up by His glory.

> *The people who walk in darkness will see a great light* **(Isaiah 9:2).**

The Without Came Upon

On mount Sinai, when the glory of God was revealed to Moses, a thick cloud also enveloped him. When he came down from the mountain, the Bible records he needed to veil himself to conceal the light of God radiating from his face.

At the dedication of Solomon's temple, found in Second Chronicles 5, we see the priests and musicians unified in worship to God. As their heartfelt praises rose, the Bible records a thick cloud filled the temple. The weight of God's Presence became so tangible, it caused the priests to literally lose physical strength. Appropriately, the Hebrew word used for *glory* in this passage is *kavod*, which can be translated "heavy weight."

> *The house of the Lord was filled with a cloud, so that the priests could not stand to minister because of*

the cloud, for the glory of the Lord filled the house of God **(2 Chronicles 5:13-14).**

Now interestingly, the same glory both Moses and the priests and musicians of Solomon encountered had varying effects. With Moses, the glory sustained his frame through a 40-day fast and raised him to life. With Solomon's people, it produced a bodily weakness. It took their natural strength. This symbolizes the bilateral relationship between the love and fear of God. Where His glory resides, so resides both a freedom and a tremble. In God's kingdom, these attributes ought to never be divorced, but eternally married. So should it be with the people of God—holy yet free.

The Without Came Within

Now, the two accounts just mentioned were from the Old Testament. They reveal the light of God reflected upon men who encountered His external glory. So, what about the New Testament? We know of Jesus' experience upon the mount of transfiguration. But what about Christ's disciples? Did His followers manifest His glory?

In the book of Acts, we see Stephen standing trial before the Sanhedrin. He'd been dragged there against his will by false witnesses and persecutors. The Bible then records:

And fixing their gaze on him, all who were sitting in the Council saw his face like the face of an angel **(Acts 6:15).**

The light of God's glory manifested upon the face of Stephen. Yet in this instance, there was no mountain. No praise and worship music preceded a heavenly cloud. In fact, Stephen would not have the open vision of heaven until one chapter later, at the end of his interaction with this council. This time, the glory that shone came from *within!* How and why did this "ordinary" believer manifest the light of God's glory?

> *Stephen, a man full of God's grace and power, performed amazing miracles and signs among the people* **(Acts 6:8 NLT).**

Stephen was not one of the 12 apostles. The Bible never even gives him a ministry "title." In fact, he was a waiter of tables (see Acts 6:1-2). Yet, Stephen was filled with the Holy Spirit. He performed mighty signs, wonders, and miracles. He walked with God in such a way that the Spirit lived not merely within him but spilled out!

Now, I'm not suggesting the only fruit of being filled with the Spirit is emanating visual light. That is merely one manifestation of His Presence. I am, however, posing the question: What is truly possible for those today filled with the Holy Spirit? Can we manifest God's glory as Stephen once did? Surely, it is so! God's Presence is not merely for the "special." While there are different roles of ministry and giftings present in the body of Christ, the invitation for encountering and facilitating His supernatural is extended to all! For even of Elijah it is written:

> *Elijah was as human as we are, and yet when he prayed earnestly that no rain would fall, none fell for three and a half years!* **(James 5:17 NLT)**

Notice, this passage was written by James (Jacob) in the New Testament. In fact, the new covenant expressly states there is *more* glory available in Christ than under Moses' covenant!

> *But if the ministry of death, in letters engraved on stones, came with glory, so that the sons of Israel could not look intently at the face of Moses because of the glory of his face, fading as it was, how will the ministry of the Spirit fail to be even more with glory? For if the ministry of condemnation has glory, much more does the ministry of righteousness abound in glory* **(2 Corinthians 3:7-9).**

Father of Lights

Contrary to what some modern religious teaching suggests, there are numerous eye-witness accounts of God's glory upon men throughout history. Take the ministry of Saint Columba, for example.

Columba was a sixth-century Irish priest. He founded several monasteries and was revered throughout much of Ireland and Scotland as a man of holiness. Columba was also renowned for walking in the power of the Holy Spirit. Many eyewitness accounts of the glory of God visibly manifesting upon him are recorded in the book *Life of St. Columba* by Adomnan of Iona. One such account is as follows:

> On another occasion when St. Columba was living in Hinba, the grace of the Holy Spirit was poured upon him in incomparable abundance and miraculously remained over him for three days. During that time, he remained day and night locked in his house, which was filled with heavenly light. No one was allowed to go near him, and he neither ate nor drank. But from the house, rays of brilliant light could be seen at night, escaping through the chinks of the doors and through the keyholes. He was also heard singing spiritual chants of a kind never heard before.[1]

So, what about us today? Since I am the one writing this book, what of His glory in my own life?

"I can't look in your eyes!" is a phrase I've heard numerous times when casting out demons. Evil spirits see in the spirit realm, after all! They know when a person is housing His Presence. What is even more encouraging to me, however, is when human beings with no grid for such things encounter the glory in our eyes!

In some of the earlier days of our Loft meetings, I would both lead worship and preach. We hadn't many other members who could do either, so I did my best to utilize both gifts until we had more help. One such night, I had just finished leading worship and set the guitar down to transition to a different part of the service. Suddenly, a first-time visitor caught eyes with me and let out a blood-curdling scream. At the top of her lungs, she cried, "Josh, I see Jesus' light in your eyes!" She then immediately fell backward to the floor, "slain in the Spirit." I was rather taken aback in the moment, because I physically felt no different than any time before. All I knew was I'd worshiped with all of my heart and needed a quick breather before stepping up to preach. Nevertheless, during my time of glorifying God, His glory began to manifest upon me!

What made this moment even more authentic was the woman on the floor was not accustomed to the manifestations of the Holy Spirit. In fact, from what we understood, she had never experienced anything like this before. Yet now she laid prostrate, tears streaming down her cheeks, under the weight of Christ's majesty. That is the power of Jesus' glory. A mere glimpse in His eyes has ability to wreck even the most skeptical hearts. God is certainly still doing these things today!

> *To whom God willed to make known what is the riches of the glory of this mystery among the Gentiles, which is Christ in you, the hope of glory* **(Colossians 1:27).**

Visions of Glory

Light is one attribute of God, but what about the Person inside the light? Is it possible to see or even talk to the resurrected Christ Himself?

When I was in college, I read many books on church history and revival. I was fascinated especially by the array of supernatural encounters that followed the lives of men and women such as Smith Wigglesworth, John G. Lake, Maria Woodworth-Etter, Kathryn Kuhlman, and more. These generals of the Holy Spirit stirred my faith and hunger for God like few others. I distinctly remember one night having a conversation with the Lord about some of the accounts I'd been reading.

"Jesus," I began, "I deeply desire to host Your Presence in these ways. If you will trust me to walk in Your Presence, I promise (as far as I'm able by Your grace) to not pull back or quench even the *stranger* things You might do—so long as they're truly from You."

I'd almost forgotten about that prayer until years later at Loft Church, when we began frequently experiencing one of the more unique yet powerful manifestations of the Holy Spirit.

> *And your young men shall see visions, and your old men shall dream dreams; even on My bondslaves, both men and women, I will in those days pour forth of My Spirit and they shall prophesy* **(Acts 2:17-18).**

I grew up believing that supernatural visions were an extremely rare event. What I didn't understand was, the greater the measure of God's glory manifesting near our lives, the greater propensity for supernatural visitation. From the moment the Holy Spirit's Presence increased in my life, people in and around our meetings began to have unique encounters in the realm of visions and trances.

Now, you might not initially associate the word *trance* with *vision*, but it turns out the two are closely interlinked in Scripture. In Acts 2, the word *vision* in the original Greek is the word *horasis* and is defined as "an appearance divinely granted in an ecstasy." Interestingly, the word *ecstasy* in Greek is *ekstasis* and is found at least twice in the New Testament. Its English translation? "Trance!" Strong's Concordance more fully defines a trance as "a displacement (of the mind), bewilderment, ecstasy." In other words, when you have a true, open vision, you almost always do so by way of a trance.

Many cultures are rich with histories of people falling into trances, though not all related to Christ. In fact, for thousands of years people have been known to seek visions by inducing trance-like states through use of extreme fasting, drugs, herbs, etc. The reason these practices have lasted for millennia anthropologically is because they often do produce compelling spiritual experiences.

Of course, from a biblical paradigm, purposely inducing such states of our own volition is forbidden (see Deut. 18:10). The Scripture is explicit that in doing so, we can open doors to the demonic realm. I've personally seen demons cast out of people who've participated in hypnosis, for example, which produces an altered state of consciousness. Obviously then, those attempting to directly commune with other types of spirits or entities are in particular danger of colluding with agents of darkness, even if they masquerade as "angels of light" (see 2 Cor. 11:14).

> *The things which the Gentiles sacrifice* **[to idols],** *they sacrifice to demons and not to God; and I do not want you to become sharers in demons* **(1 Corinthians 10:20).**

That said, visions and trances originally belong to Jesus! They are first His creation and idea, and in communing with the Holy Spirit, they are one way we encounter the glory of God today. The fine line between pure and impure, divine and divination is the source of initiation. When initiated by the Spirit of Christ, visions and trances are quite scriptural, legal for believers to experience, and oftentimes result in fruit of the gospel being advanced. (See Addendum section for more criteria on "discerning good from evil spirits.")

The Bible records in Acts 10 that Peter fell into a trance while praying on the roof of Simon the Tanner's house in Joppa. This resulted in a heavenly vision, communicating to him through symbols that God had made a way for the Gentiles to receive the gospel. In Acts 22, Paul falls into a trance while praying in Jerusalem's temple. His trance, too, produced a vision, whereby the Lord Jesus Himself spoke and gave Paul specific instructions for his next mission.

During our regular services, it is now not uncommon to find someone freezing in place for long periods of time during worship. One man, Faron Jourdan, was once recorded as being in a suspended state to such a degree, his eyes didn't blink for over half an hour. Faron's wife, Cathy, has often been seen worshiping before falling into a suspended state with eyes rapidly flickering. Another woman, Julia Waddell, has a handful of times had her body frozen in unusual positions. When she'd "come to," she'd have prophetic instructions for individuals or the direction of the meeting at large.

I believe it's important to note that when these encounters began occurring in our meetings, our leadership chose to honor them as holy. I'm convinced this is one reason why they've not only continued, but to my pleasant surprise, increased in frequency and intensity. The Lord seems pleased to multiply that which we honor, and I am abundantly grateful for His doing so.

I See the Lord

Most awe inspiring to me are those trances which have produced direct encounters with our Jesus Himself.

On one occasion, a small ministry team of our leaders was praying for a woman named Tori. In prior years, Tori had walked with the Lord and had a robust relationship with Him. However, she'd recently grown discouraged about the season of life she was in. This resulted in her falling back into a life of sin, especially in relationships with men. She was now truly repentant, though, and wanted to reestablish an authentic walk with Christ.

After listening to Tori share her shortcomings with godly sorrow, we led her through a few simple prayers of repentance. Then, we began to speak words of forgiveness, life, and self-worth over her. Now, often in these moments, the Holy Spirit begins to work alongside our Word-based declarations and "laying on of hands" prayer. We've seen many powerful encounters with God's love, healing, and even deliverance over the years while doing this very thing. This time, however, nothing seemed to be happening.

For a few minutes, we pressed in a little further. Still, the room felt empty of His familiar Presence and resulting fruit. Suddenly, I heard the Holy Spirit whisper distinctly, "These have all been nice prayers, son. Are you ready to do what I want now?"

In that moment, I realized we'd made the classic mistake of allowing even our normally Spirit-filled ministry to become formulaic, based on successes of the past. After inwardly acknowledging the Lord's correction, I gently instructed our team to step back. I said, "Guys, let's give the Lord some room to minister to Tori however He chooses. I think He may want to do something special here."

Tori remained in the middle, her head bowed and eyes closed, while each of our team backed away several feet to quietly wait on the Holy Spirit. Only a few seconds later, Tori collapsed to the floor as if dead. I took a step in to check and make sure she was okay, when I heard the Lord once more. He lovingly but sternly said, "This one is Mine, son. Don't touch her." Like an outranked soldier before a commanding officer, I humbly responded, "Yes, Sir," and backed off again.

We waited in silence for several minutes before Tori suddenly seemed to come to a state of consciousness. When she did, she began weeping, yet with bouts of laughter in the middle. With dry remnants of streaming mascara upon her cheeks, she cried out, "Oh, Jesus! Thank You! Thank You!"

Finally, Tori stood up, looked at us, and shouted. "I saw Jesus! I literally saw Him! He talked to me about my life. He even told me if I'd wait patiently for a short time more, He'd bring the man I was to marry!"

We all stood in awe. Tori left that day a renewed woman, cleansed, as if she'd never sinned. The Lord had explained His forgiveness to her in a way that removed all doubt from her heart. She was free once more and filled with hope for her future. No more than a year later, she did meet that man of her dreams!

> *Now return to the Lord your God, for He is gracious and compassionate* **(Joel 2:13).**

Grace upon Grace

One of the people in our congregation who has repeatedly experienced the most profound visions is Grace Alexander. Grace first began attending the Loft as part of a young adults group meeting in my apartment. She initially stood out as more academically minded but hungering for the things of the Holy Spirit. Though she was familiar with the concept of the third member of the Godhead, she'd not encountered much of His Presence yet in ways described in this book.

However, within weeks of Grace's coming, the Lord began moving mightily upon her and in transformative ways. One of the first changes was her heart seemed to grow extremely tender to the Presence of Jesus. Oftentimes, she couldn't make it through a single worship song or reading of the Scripture before profusely weeping. She had fallen madly in love with the King.

Soon after, the trances began. For a season, these experiences became so regular, we'd sometimes not even finish giving preliminary meeting announcements before her body would be frozen with eyes flickering. These encounters would sometimes last for a few minutes, while other times for the duration of the entire evening. I personally was witness to Grace having once been caught up in a trance for over 18 consecutive hours. Toward the end of that encounter, she tried relaying the heavenly things she'd seen, but every time she began talking about Jesus, she'd fall into a trance again. It was as if she was suspended between two worlds. For a day, God allowed her to be as familiar with the unseen as the seen.

Perhaps the most powerful vision Grace received (to date) occurred near the end of one of our Sunday evening services. The altar that night had been especially weighty, and many were lingering in worship near the front of the stage. Suddenly, something seemed to shift in the atmosphere and many men and women began weeping. That weeping then turned to loud wails and groaning (see Rom. 8:26).

At the same moment, two or three of our women fell into trance-like states, either lying prostrate on the carpet or freezing in place while standing. With both arms raised nearly chest high, like a classical Greek sculpture, Grace stood utterly suspended. This time, however, a look of awe consumed her face. Both her eyes and mouth were wide open, as if she were seeing something immensely terrifying.

Moments later, she began repeating the words over and over, "He's here. He's holy! He's here. He's holy." Her body trembled as tears streamed down her frozen cheeks. The room grew silent. Those few left standing began falling involuntarily to the floor. Jesus had walked in the room. Grace literally saw Him. This time, though, He came in the same form apostle John had seen in the book of Revelation—a Man of fire.

> *His eyes were like a flame of fire. ... When I saw him, I fell at His feet like a dead man* **(Revelation 1:14,17).**

Not only did these encounters produce a new reverence for the majesty and holiness of Christ in Grace, but after one such vision of His glory, she was supernaturally healed of a chronic digestive disorder! When Jesus walks into the room, truly everything changes.

Many other nights at the Loft the glory of God has fallen so heavily upon the room, no one can remain standing. At times, visitors have even come late to the meetings, walked in the door, and immediately fallen to the ground under the weight of His glory. In these moments, some people weep and wail. Other times, waves of laughter and ecstasy break forth. One of our leaders, Tammy Chambliss, has often smelled heavenly (yet naturally absent) fragrances, such as flowers, honey, or peppermint. Some have even seen or physically felt the presence of angels. I'm convinced on one occasion I personally walked into one! It knocked me back with such a force, it felt as though I'd run into an invisible brick wall. Words cannot express my gratitude for God allowing us to experience Him in these ways. The God of glory longs to be with His children, and indeed He is.

> *The Lord gives grace and glory; no good thing does He withhold from those who walk uprightly* **(Psalm 84:11).**

Note

1. Adomnan of Iona, *Life of St. Columba* (London: Penguin Books, 1995), 219-220.

CHAPTER 15

UNION WITH GOD

Moments of supernatural encounter are wonderful and wildly fruitful. But what is the ultimate purpose of such manifestations in human beings? Is it merely to testify of Christ's existence, or does our God have more in mind? Certainly, revealing Christ is of the highest order of kingdom significance, but what if in God's manifold wisdom, He were also desiring to show the world a greater potential—a lifestyle He intended for His people to walk in from the beginning?

Interestingly, secular science now demonstrates compelling evidence that all human beings may have lying dormant a potential far beyond that with which most are familiar. One field of study especially intriguing in this regard involves brain injuries. Readers may be familiar with *savant syndrome*. In *congenital savant syndrome*, extraordinary abilities usually surface in early childhood. Perhaps you've read an article or television show depicting a savant possessing genius level mathematical or musical talents. The popular movie *Rain Man*, for example, portrayed the life of Kim Peek, a savant with extraordinary memory.

Unfortunately, as with many savants, Peek was deficient in other areas of brain function and social interaction. In fact, about 50 percent of *congenital savant* cases are today associated with autism or the autistic subtype, Asperger's syndrome. Many researchers have postulated that in such cases, one part of the brain seems to "overcompensate" for a lesser functioning part. With *congenital savants*, one could say they received the blessing or cursing (depending on one's view) of probability. Out of the spectrum of humanity, some by mathematical chance end up on extreme ends of the distribution.[1]

However, there is another type of savant syndrome recently discovered which has opened an entirely new list of questions as to the potential of *all* human beings. In *acquired savants*, staggering new abilities appear in an ordinary person after a head injury, trauma to the brain, or central nervous system. Prior to such injuries these abilities were nonexistent.

Take the case of Orlando Serrell. At age 10, Orlando was hit in the head by a baseball. Soon afterward, he acquired an uncanny ability to quickly name the day that a given date (of any year) falls upon. Orlando has also been able to remember the specific weather for each day since his accident. In addition, he developed "hyperthymestic syndrome," which includes the capacity to recall precisely what he did on a particular day following his injury.

Another fascinating case of *acquired savant syndrome* can be found in the book *Born on a Blue Day*. This autobiography details the life of Daniel Tammet, an otherwise normal man who as a child suffered from a form of epilepsy, resulting in a series of severe seizures. Immediately following, Daniel began to experience a unique synesthesia in which every number has its own color, shape, and texture. Like Orlando Serrell, Daniel also acquired an aptitude for calendar calculation. In Daniel's case, though, he developed a remarkable memory for massive number sequences as well, including pi (3.14) to 22,514 decimal places! If that weren't enough, Daniel has been observed learning entirely new languages within just one week.[2]

These are but a few of a handful of extraordinary cases of *acquired savant syndrome* documented in recent years. In addition to uncanny memorization, others with this condition have instantaneous acumen for master-level classical music performance, painting, sculpting, and more.[3]

What can account for the sudden onset of these genius abilities in previously ordinary individuals? What does this unique syndrome suggest? Many scientists have postulated that every human being may have a significant percentage of their brain function "locked up" with capabilities far beyond what history has generally regarded as normal. But these seemingly dormant genius skill sets would seem to work against an evolutionary premise of survival of the fittest. Nature's "killing them off" would have placed us at greater disadvantage, rather than advantage. On the contrary, these missing parts would have surely propelled humanity's progress forward. It's as if something far superior was once present in humanity's being, but now has been lost—and perhaps that's precisely the truth of the matter.

I'd like to propose that in the garden of Eden, Adam and Eve walked in a fuller measure of God's created intent for the whole being. They had greater access to divine understandings of music, arts, and language. They could process things on a much higher level of intelligence—God's wavelength, if you will. Remember, they were created in the image of God, and there was no death in them, as sin had no hold over them.

So, what if in the fall of man, amidst sin's cursed effects, many parts of the human being were "powered off"—abilities which, among other things, allowed us to perceive and commune with the mind of Christ? And what if then, by way of Christ's atonement and rebirthing of man, our garden state of being has once again become accessible? What if that communication link can be reestablished by way of the Holy Spirit?

> In the beginning, man's spirit was the dominant force in the world. When he sinned, his mind became dominant. Sin dethroned the spirit and crowned the intellect. But grace is restoring the spirit to its place of dominion. When man comes to realize this, he will live in the realm of the supernatural without effort. —John G. Lake

I believe this is precisely God's goal for us in Christ! The Scripture seems to indicate quite clearly that through continual yielding to the Holy Spirit, we can now enter a terrific discernment of heavenly things—chiefly, God's mind.

> *But solid food is for the mature, who because of practice have their senses trained to discern good and evil* **(Hebrews 5:14).**
>
> *For who among men knows the thoughts of a man except the spirit of the man which is in him? Even so the thoughts of God no one knows except the Spirit of God. Now we have received, not the spirit of the world, but the Spirit who is from God, so that we may know the things freely given to us by God. ...For who has known the mind of the Lord, that he will instruct Him? But we have the mind of Christ* **(1 Corinthians 2:11-12,16).**

Spirit-Acquired Language

One of my good friends in the Lord, Joel Tenney, has become regularly accustomed to one such *acquired* super-ability—xenoglossia. Joel grew up in a Russian orthodox sect of Christianity. From the time he was a child, he was intensely trained in the Scriptures and church history for the purpose of becoming an orthodox priest. Joel's sect, however, did not hold to the doctrines of salvation by grace through faith. Neither did they believe in the present-day *charismata* (supernatural power, gifts the Holy Spirit, etc.).

That is, until one day while searching the Scriptures, the Holy Spirit illuminated to him his need for salvation through faith in the blood of Jesus. Joel recognized rituals and liturgical practices couldn't atone for his sins. He bowed his knee to Christ and asked Him to enter. Not only did Jesus receive Joel's prayer, but He baptized him in the Holy Spirit with the evidence of speaking in tongues at the same time! Quickly, the Lord called him to an evangelistic ministry accompanied by signs, wonders, and miracles.

One such instance of Joel being used in a miraculous "unlocking" of the mind of Christ occurred near his hometown in Minnesota. One day, he was in Lakeville (a suburb of Minneapolis) and spotted a Somalian man and his family walking across the street. Joel felt a strong prophetic impression from the Lord that at least two of the man's close relatives were ill back in Somalia. Upon approaching the man in faith, Joel began to feel a distinct tingling sensation on the tip of his tongue. When Joel reached the man, he attempted to relay the prophetic message in English, but when he opened his mouth, he instead began to speak another language altogether. For several minutes, Joel spoke by faith to the Somalian man through this unknown tongue.

When he finished speaking, the man stood stunned. He responded, "How did you come to learn my native language of Somali? Also, how did you know this information about my relatives?!"

The prophetic word Joel gave was not only accurate, but the Holy Spirit had conveyed it in such a miraculous way, the Somalian Muslim man immediately repented of his sins and received Jesus Christ as Lord and Savior!

As astounding as this story is, it's by no means an isolated tale. Joel has to date spoken in over 26 unknown languages by way of the Holy Spirit! He has video documentation and firsthand testimonials of many of these occurrences. I have seen them with my own eyes!

Theosis (Spiritual Transformation)

In Eastern Orthodox traditions, there is a concept or doctrine often unfamiliar to 21st-century Protestants. It's called *theosis*. Theosis, or deification, as it may also be referred to, is defined as "the transformative process of man into His likeness to or union with God."

Now, to some that may sound an alarming proposition. Are we talking about ourselves becoming deity? Certainly not. There is but one God, represented in three Persons. That will never change. The concept of theosis, however, is to become unified through relationship with that One God to such a degree that we begin to take on His divine energies and attributes. This may seem a foreign concept to some in the western church, but it is precisely what the Scripture teaches in many ways!

> *Seeing that His divine power has granted to us everything pertaining to life and godliness,*

> *through the true knowledge of Him who called us by His own glory and excellence. For by these He has granted to us His precious and magnificent promises, so that by them you may become partakers of the divine nature, having escaped the corruption that is in the world by lust* **(2 Peter 1:3-4).**

We are invited into this union with God through His divine power. By faith, we receive grace to enter the precious promises offered as an inheritance to those in Christ Jesus. That inheritance includes blood-bought access to the Throne of God through communion with the Holy Spirit. And as we abide in that fellowship, we begin to share in His divine nature, enabling us to live in holiness.

Several years ago, while battling chronic sickness, I visited a hormone specialist in Kansas. His treatments didn't help my condition at the time, but something he demonstrated about the human body made an impact on me in more ways than one. The specialist explained that our skin is far more absorbent than most people are aware. The body takes in and processes the substances of our environments in many ways. He demonstrated this by placing a solitary drop of a chemical compound on my wrist. Then he asked, "what do you taste?"

Before he finished his sentence, I had a powerfully bitter, metallic taste in my mouth. The molecules from that substance had traveled through the various layers of my skin, into my bloodstream, reaching the taste buds of my tongue in less than three seconds!

The reality is, this is not only a physical process, but a spiritual one as well. We are sponges. We absorb our environments: the sounds, images, and words around us—whether of good or of evil.

> *The eye is the lamp of the body. So if your eye is good, your whole body will be full of light. But if your eye is evil, your whole body will be full of darkness. Therefore, if the light within you has turned into darkness, how great is that darkness* **(Matthew 6:22-23 NKJV).**

We must be careful what we put ourselves before on a regular basis. Too much time amidst things of the world only results in the world seeping in. I don't mean to suggest hyper-avoidance of the world in general, as we'd then cease engaging them as Christ (see 1 Cor 5:9-10). Rather, it is the continual and willful submitting of ourselves to worldly things that becomes problematic (see Ps. 1:1). However, if we choose to spend our time abiding in Christ's light, we will absorb His light. We will become it. Then, we will emit it for all the world to see! Our time is valuable. Our minds and bodies are precious gifts. God beckons us to use these tools as He always intended: to become one with Him—to become heaven's thin place on the earth.

> *If we walk in the Light as He Himself is in the Light, we have fellowship with one another, and the blood of Jesus His Son cleanses us from all sin. ... The one who says he abides in Him ought himself to walk in the same manner as He walked* **(1 John 1:7; 2:6).**

To be holy doesn't merely mean to live without sin. No, sinlessness is a symptom of holiness, but it is not the totality of its reality. *Holiness* means quite literally "to be set apart." That is, to have been removed from one reality and placed into another. That other reality is the kingdom of heaven. It is our true home, and we are intended to become increasingly unified with it starting here and now!

> *Now the Lord is the Spirit, and where the Spirit of the Lord is, there is liberty. But we all, with unveiled face, beholding as in a mirror the glory of the Lord, are being transformed into the same image from glory to glory, just as from the Lord, the Spirit* **(2 Corinthians 3:17-18).**

Now, the word *transformed* in this passage in the original Greek is *metamorphoo.* It means to change into another form. From this word, we derive the modern English word *metamorphosis.* If you're thinking of a caterpillar-to-butterfly analogy, you're on the right track! The Scripture takes this to another depth of understanding, though. *Metamorphoo* is also precisely the same word used in describing Jesus' transfiguration on the mountain! With that in mind, let's look one more time at verse 18.

> *But we all, with unveiled face, beholding as in a mirror the glory of the Lord, are being* **(transformed)** *into the same image from glory to glory* **(2 Corinthians 3:18).**

When we read it like that, our "transformation" seems to carry greater weight! As we commune and abide with Christ, we are *transfigured* into the same glorious substance He bore before Peter, James, and John on the mountain (see Matt. 17)! This is also why Stephen's face shone before his accusers. It wasn't because he was on a mountain. It was because his true, inward colors were showing. Stephen had cultivated a life of intimacy with Christ residing *within*. Christ's glory then lit him up for all to see! Stephen exhibited symptoms of the same *theosis* made available to us!

Now, strict textualists may argue the "glory to glory" in Second Corinthians 3:18 is in reference to the contextual contrast Paul previously makes between the old covenant and the new (see 2 Cor. 3:7-8). I will concede that is partly true. But then, I've found strict textualists seem to rarely understand the layered, prophetic nature of Scripture, let alone walk in depths of the Spirit.

Of course, the finished nature of our spirits is theologically representative of the new covenant's greater glory. However, the Scripture also attests to the simultaneous, progressive nature of our transformation into Christ's likeness. We go from faith to faith (see Rom. 1:17). We are continually renewed in minds and bodies (see Rom. 12:1-3). We undergo a process of soulish sanctification as we abide in His Word and Presence (see 1 Thess. 5:23; Phil. 2:12-13). These are not either/or realities, but both/and—two sides of the same coin.

Now, many religions suggest a strictly linear path of "illumination" to achieve union with the divine. Not so with biblical Christianity. Rather, Jesus often multitasks our relational growth with Him. Due to Christ's atoning work and the indwelling gift of the Holy Spirit, we can commune with the living God on day one of our salvation, despite lacking maturity in other aspects of our walk. The goal is spiritual growth through relationship, rather than growth to achieve it. The Bible says we go from "glory to glory," not "nothing to glory." We start at glory! Therefore, our new covenant identity is for the very purpose of leading us into progressive intimacy with our Savior!

The prospect of union with God should also not be equated with becoming a strangely aloof, unapproachable person. This is where I believe some parishioners of this doctrine have in the past gotten off. Jesus was more in union with the Father than anyone in history, and yet He was approachable. Christ was sociable, even regularly embracing the company of children. Only, He would then regularly return to isolated places to be alone with the Father. In short, Jesus prayed, and Jesus went. A true follower of Christ must also learn to balance both realities.

Moreover, remember that prayer is not sitting legalistically in a broom closet, attempting to hum and chant our way into a spiritual state. No, prayer is to be a two-way love affair. We enter communion by grace through faith! That's the beholding of Him. This is a progressive journey, and we are to enjoy increasingly becoming one with Him by the Spirit, whereby we begin exhibiting transfigured attributes of His holiness.

Comm + Unity

Union with God is not only intended to be an individual reality, but communal also. The individual certainly is vital, but Christ died not merely for distinct individuals, but for His church! He intends for us to in many ways function as one!

> *The cup of blessing which we bless, is it not the communion of the blood of Christ? The bread which we break, is it not the communion of the body of Christ? For we, though many, are one bread and one body; for we all partake of that one bread* **(1 Corinthians 10:16-17 NKJV).**

This passage speaks about the sacrament of taking holy bread and water, and it also symbolizes God's desire for the church to function together unified in Him.

My friend and fellow minister Bo Salisbury aptly sums up this reality of community in saying, "Paul brings revelation to the representation of the bread, not just to the literal body of Jesus that was broken for us on Calvary, but to the body of Christ, the church. Jesus was the body of Christ. But now the church is the body of Christ according to Scripture. Christ dwells in us. We are the house of the Lord. He lives in us. We are one bread and one body. If we want to experience the fullness of kingdom culture in our lives, we must migrate from individualism to true community, represented by true communion that includes fully engaging with both Christ and the body of Christ. One without the other just won't do."

> *In whom the whole building, being fitted together, is growing into a holy temple in the Lord, in whom you also are being built together into a dwelling of God in the Spirit* **(Ephesians 2:21-22).**

It is true there is a far surpassing glory in the third heaven when we die, but not all in the church have realized their supernatural empowerment and purpose while living! Jesus wants to remedy that by illuminating to us many overlooked aspects of His Word, especially the aspect of becoming one with Him.

> *The glory which You have given Me I have given to them, that they may be one, just as We are one; I in them and You in Me, that they may be perfected in unity, so that the world may know that You sent Me, and loved them, even as You have loved Me* **(John 17:22-23).**

The *same* glory? The same!? Jesus literally prays we'd come into the very same union with heaven that He enjoyed in this life. Think of the possibilities! If there were ever any doubt as to whether theosis were God's will, this passage ought to seal the deal! Jesus then prays the world would know our unity by the glory we carry, the very same He shared on this earth with God the Father. If this were speaking of an age to come, what benefit would the world derive from knowing about it? Rather, Jesus prays here that His followers sharing the same glory He and His Father did would be a sign to the world that Christ was the One true offering sent from heaven!

We are God's sign to the world. When the world sees a church that talks and walks like Christ, they are more compelled to believe in Him. We aren't to wait until death to know and emanate the effects of our union with God. His nature ought to be evident in and through us here, now. Death isn't our Savior. Jesus is!

> *For the law of the Spirit of life in Christ Jesus has set you free from the law of sin and of death* **(Romans 8:2).**

Attracting Heaven Here

On a recent autumn day while on vacation in Colorado, I visited a chiropractor for a simple adjustment. I'd never met this man, but being aware some in chiropractic practice employ spiritual methodologies outside of a Christian framework, I prayed for the Lord's Presence to envelop and protect me during the treatment. How God answered that short prayer reminded me once again how close He really is!

After brief introductions, the chiropractor invited me to lie on his worktable facing up. As he picked up my arm to begin examination, suddenly the glory of God began manifesting all over my body. A wave of the Spirit's fire swept through me so profoundly, I began sweating through my shirt. Within moments, the chiropractor became so overwhelmed with that same supernatural Presence, he began profusely shaking. For a few more moments, he attempted to continue examining me, but it was no use. He nearly fell on top of my body before finally stepped back. With his hands covering his mouth, he stuttered, "I can't even...I don't know what to do with you." He continued, "What is happening to me? I'm laughing. I'm crying. I feel intoxicated with what I can only describe as overwhelming love. Such a peace is surging out of you, I feel heavy all over."

When I explained it was the Presence of Jesus, He replied, "In eight years of practice, seeing up to 12 patients a day, I've never experienced anything like this." Knowing this wonder was to further reveal Christ's gospel and goodness, I made sure to relay the message to the chiropractor.

Shortly after, I was reminded of Jesus' promise, "*Whoever has my commandments and keeps them, he it is who loves me. And he who loves me will be loved by my Father, and I will love him and manifest myself to him"* (John 14:21 ESV). Oh, what is truly possible if we'll simply abide and obey!

Now I'm not suggesting I have "arrived." In this miraculous journey, I have neither been the perfect person nor pastor. My church, ministry friends, and acquaintances are not perfect people either. We have all made mistakes along the way, and Jesus has extended mercy in the process.

But this I know for certain: If we want to attract heaven, we must believe His Word above all else. We must allow it to shape us, to mold us into that which God desires. Concerning communion with the Spirit, whether individually or corporately, we must be willing to allow God to do anything He desires to do in our midst. "Come, Holy Spirit," if merely words, is not enough. We must mean these words with all our hearts. We must submit our plans, our agendas, yes, even our lives to His ways. We must receive His "foolishness" to gain His wisdom (see 1 Cor. 1:27). In relinquishing our carnal hand of control, we invite His masterful Hand to take over. That is the humble posture from which heaven will invade earth.

Eavesdropping God

Such was the appearance of the likeness of the glory of the Lord. And when I saw it, I fell on my face and heard a voice speaking **(Ezekiel 1:28).**

Perhaps the most unique account of divine union I've personally witnessed involved overhearing a real-time conversation between God and a woman in our church. Another Sunday evening at our church had gone well into the midnight hours, as several people lay in the altar encountering the Holy Spirit. That night, a woman named Tina McCluskie had gone into a trance, but instead of being frozen in place—as we'd grown accustomed to seeing—her body was seemingly being jolted by surges of spiritual power while lying on her back. Every few moments, Tina's eyes would flicker, and she would softly scream as if on an invisible roller coaster ride. As she would cry out, her head and feet would raise off the ground a few inches in a kind of "abdomen crunch."

Though it appeared bizarre in the natural, the Lord gave me wisdom to discern at least some of what Tina was experiencing. After coming out of the encounter, she corroborated my thoughts by saying, "It felt like I was flying through space with the Holy Spirit before landing somewhere to converse."

That night, after a few moments of these "supernatural traveling" experiences, Tina began to whisper out loud. I moved in closer while switching on my phone's audio recorder. With her eyes still flickering, I could hear Tina was having an audible, two-way conversation with someone. It was the Lord! He would talk through her mouth (which we could hear), and she would then respond to Him out loud. He was sharing with her His plans for the church at large.

Suddenly, the Holy Spirit said through Tina's mouth, "Josh, Josh. Come closer."

In reverence of the moment, I leaned in. He continued, "I've been watching you, son. You've been faithful. I will give My glory to My faithful ones. It's going to happen. All those things you've heard. All those things you've read. It's coming, son—in a greater measure than you've known."

The Lord then whispered a few personal things to me that I will always cherish. Before concluding, He said, "And you will write about this. You will write about My glory."

Afterward, the Lord called a few more people in the room by name through Tina, and they too came near to hear God speak over their own life. That night, Tina's husband, Jeff, had to carry her to their car. She was in and out of the Spirit so much, she didn't fully come back to her earthly awareness until the next day!

Although God sometimes chooses the most seemingly unlikely of candidates to reveal Himself, other times He chooses the most faithful. Jeff and Tina McCluskie certainly would qualify as the latter, and I'll always be thankful for their life example and for allowing God to use them so uniquely.

Amen

An End for a New Beginning

If your relationship with God has ever felt lacking or perhaps your hope of connection with Him altogether lost, I pray this book will serve as a notice of its finding.

The chief inspiration I hope to impart to those reading is that to walk in love, freedom, and fellowship with God—to experience His miraculous Presence, power, and intimate union—is not an unattainable ideal. Both the Scriptures and the Holy Spirit attest time and again that an earthly lifestyle of heavenly habitation is not only possible, but God's very intent for everyone! Jesus has not reserved this glory for a select super-elite. No, He wants us all to explore the possibilities of His divine union. He cheerleads us not merely from heavenly places, but He has sent His Spirit to guide, encourage, and comfort us from within, amidst our progressive journey from glory to glory on the earth.

God's manifest Presence is found at the nexus of the Spirit within and the Spirit upon. Through consistent faith, worship, intimacy, and grace-fueled obedience, we become the thin place, the intersection between heaven and earth. The Holy Spirit of Glory is God's gift to the church and hosting Him well results in revealing Christ to a world in need.

> *For the earth will be filled with the knowledge of the glory of the Lord, as the waters cover the sea* **(Habakkuk 2:14).**

What will be said of you beyond death? After your mortal coil has been burned or buried, will the world recall a lifestyle of selfish pursuits and finite achievements, or will your name echo for generations as one who faithfully revealed Christ? The latter endeavor requires faith. It requires radical shifts in thinking. It will at times be perilous, resulting in seasons of hardship and suffering. Nevertheless, as Christ be eternal, His pursuit is the only meaning worth living.

God's glory is our inheritance. It is our purpose. His kingdom is within reach. With an extended hand, Jesus invites each of us to follow Him into the glories of heaven here, before the hereafter. Will you respond to His call? Will you choose to believe the *more* is possible in and through your life? I pray you will.

> *Jesus said to him, "...All things are possible to him who believes"* **(Mark 9:23).**

Notes

1. Darold A. Treffert, "The savant syndrome: an extraordinary condition. A synopsis: past, present, future," Philosophical Transactions of the Royal Society B: Biological Sciences, 364(1522): 1351–1357, May 27, 2009, https://www.ncbi.nlm.nih.gov/pmc/articles/PMC2677584.

2. Darold A. Treffert, "Brain Gain: A Person Can Instantly Blossom into a Savant—and No One Knows Why," *Scientific American*, July 25, 2018, https://blogs.scientificamerican.com/observations/brain-gain-a-person-can-instantly-blossom-into-a-savant-and-no-one-knows-why/.

3. "Savant Syndrome," SSMHealth.com, accessed December 12, 2021, https://www.ssmhealth.com/treffert-center/conditions-treatments/savant-syndrome.

IMPARTATION

For I long to see you so that I may impart some spiritual gift to you, that you may be established **(Romans 1:11).**

I want to pray for you. Find a quiet place and moment to focus on the Lord. Now, receive this with humility and faith:

> Father, I pray now for those with sincere hunger for the things spoken about in this book—that which You've said in Your Word and through the testimony of my life—I pray You'd fill them now with the power of the Holy Spirit! In the name of Jesus, receive greater revelation and insight from His Word, more passion for prayer and intimacy with the Holy Spirit, and fire and glory of heaven for greater miraculous works. May increased grace of signs and wonders follow your ministry of the gospel from this day forward. Amen!

ADDENDUM

The supernatural can sometimes be difficult to accept for those unfamiliar with it. Most of us are in some measure brought up and trained in the rational ways of the world. While natural wisdom certainly exists, the book of James warns us that it's reasonings alone are not sufficient. They are even quite dangerous at times.

> *This wisdom is not that which comes down from above, but is earthly, natural, demonic* **(James 3:15).**

Now, this is not to suggest all things supernatural are pure, as from Christ. No doubt, some reading a book about *heaven here* will be skeptical, even frustrated as it confronts some theological presuppositions they've perhaps long held.

I wanted to include a brief addendum to this book to address some of these concerns, chiefly the topic of spiritual discernment. I believe the Scripture provides clear and precise criteria to determine good from evil, so that we may be assured of that which belongs to God and that which belongs to the devil.

This Is How We Distinguish

In differentiating between good and evil spirits, these are the criteria the Scripture employs:

1. Does the person or spirit confess Jesus came in the flesh and as Lord? (See 1 John 4:1-3; 1 Corinthians 12:4-5.)
2. What name does the person or spirit come in or pray by—Jesus or otherwise? (See Mark 9:38-40; Acts 19:15.)
3. What (long-term) fruit does the person or spirit bear? (See Matthew 7:16; Philippians 1:11; John 15:7-8; Galatians 5:22-23.)

True and False Works

The number-one objection opponents of the supernatural in the past have offered is a warning of "false teachers" or "false prophets." They may also speak of "lying signs and wonders." Initial caution regarding these terms is biblically founded, as all three phrases do appear in the Scripture. They must, however, be read in proper context. In order to qualify as warnings which are spiritually "false," specific biblical criteria are required.

First, let's look at the passage referring to "lying signs and wonders," in order to grasp its appropriate context:

> *Let no one in any way deceive you, for it will not come unless the apostasy comes first, and the man of lawlessness is revealed, the son of destruction, who opposes and exalts himself above every so-called god or object of worship, so that he takes his seat in the temple of God, displaying himself as being God.*
>
> *...For the mystery of lawlessness is already at work; only he who now restrains will do so until he is taken out of the way. Then that lawless one will be revealed whom the Lord will slay with the breath of His mouth and bring to an end by the appearance of His coming; that is, the one whose coming is in accord with the activity of Satan, with all power and signs and false wonders, and with all the deception of wickedness for those who perish, because they did not receive the love of the truth so as to be saved* **(2 Thessalonians 2:3-4,7-10).**

In this passage, Paul warns about a coming apostasy. But is he broadly speaking of Christian proponents of the supernatural? Absolutely not! He's specifically speaking about a *man of lawlessness* who will come and exalt himself above all known gods, declaring himself the one true and highest.

The word repeatedly used as the descriptor of this individual is *lawless*.

Now, depending on one's eschatology, this man's greater identity varies. Some believe this is speaking of an end-of-days antichrist figure. Others maintain this was historically fulfilled through one of Rome's generals during the sack of Jerusalem near A.D. 70. Either way, what is universally certain is that this description does not apply to a sincere Christ follower. Quite the contrary, it can only contextually apply to one who has rejected Christ and His gospel. The "lying signs," as it were, then do not/will not come from Christ-proclaiming believers, but from one or more outside the camp of God.

Likewise, in passages such as Matthew 24, where Jesus warns of false prophets and false christs, the context is those who claim themselves as the Messiah, or at least another god in rebellion to the exclusivity of the gospel of Jesus Christ. Once again, these warnings do not apply to sincere believers with peripheral Christian theologies differing from ours, but to those who'd deem themselves Christ or point to another altogether.

Another Scripture sometimes used to dissuade believers from supernatural works of the Holy Spirit is found in the book of First John.

> *Beloved, do not believe every spirit, but test the spirits to see whether they are from God* **(1 John 4:1).**

The problem in isolating this warning is the very next verses qualify exactly *how* to test the spirits! That would seem rather obvious, but it's often dismissed, nonetheless. When we look at verses 2 and 3, we discover a very precise criteria for testing spirits.

> *By this you know the Spirit of God: every spirit that confesses that Jesus Christ has come in the flesh is from God; and every spirit that does not confess Jesus is not from God; this is the spirit of the antichrist, of which you have heard that it is coming, and now it is already in the world* **(1 John 4:2-3).**

So, the most direct criterion for discerning spirits is identifying what they do with Jesus! Do they believe He came in the flesh as God (gnostic heresies do not), was crucified, physically rose as Lord of all, etc.? If so, the spirit isn't of the devil but of God.

Similarly, in Mark 9:38-40, Jesus made a statement with strong implications for spiritual discernment. In this passage, the disciples were flustered by a man performing miracles in Jesus' name who wasn't also a part of their direct company. What was Jesus' response to this? Did He shout, "That man is a heretic, a false prophet! He's performing lying signs and wonders." On the contrary, Jesus supported the man's work!

> *But Jesus said, "Do not hinder him, for there is no one who will perform a miracle in My name, and be able soon afterward to speak evil of Me. For he who is not against us is for us"* **(Mark 9:39-40).**

Wow! That's quite a statement. So then, another revealed biblical criteria for spiritual discernment is asking the question, "What name do they come in/perform a miracle in?" If it's in Jesus' name, it becomes rather difficult to pronounce them "false."

This also ought to silence those broadly accusing true Christian miracle workers as "kundalini" carriers. Kundalini is an eastern spirit, within the Hindu tradition. It is not "slipping into the church" under the guise of Jesus' name, lest we contradict the words of Jesus Himself. This is not to say Christians can't have demons, but they're not imparting them by invoking Jesus' name. To boot, Christ makes it clear that when we sincerely ask the God of Israel for something holy, we will not receive something unholy.

> *Now suppose one of you fathers is asked by his son for a fish; he will not give him a snake instead of a fish, will he? Or if he is asked for an egg, he will not give him a scorpion, will he? If you then, being evil, know how to give good gifts to your children, how much more will your heavenly Father give the Holy Spirit to those who ask Him?* **(Luke 11:11-13)**

We can have confidence that when we ask of God in Jesus' name, we will receive of God in Jesus' name. Moreover, when we perform a miracle in Jesus' name, the miracle will be performed by Jesus.

What About Fruit?

Now, someone might ask, "What about Jesus' warning of false prophets in sheep's clothing, mentioned in Matthew 7?" He says:

> *Many will say to Me on that day, "Lord, Lord, did we not prophesy in Your name, and in Your name cast out demons, and in Your name perform many miracles?" And then I will declare to them, "I never knew you; depart from Me, you who practice lawlessness"* **(Matthew 7:22-23).**

Before drawing sweeping conclusions from this passage, it'd be wise to first acknowledge once more Jesus' words in Mark.

> *But Jesus said, "Do not hinder him, for there is no one who will perform a miracle in My name, and be able soon afterward to speak evil of Me"* **(Mark 9:39).**

A surface level juxtaposition of this passage and that of Matthew 7 would suggest blatant contradiction. On one hand, Jesus says to accept those who do miracles in His name. On the other, He seems to suggest the opposite. What's happening here?

Well, rest assured Jesus isn't contradicting Himself. The only alternative explanation is that there is more to one of these verses than meets the eye. Being that His declaration in Mark seems rather precise to the context of miracles, it would suggest Matthew 7's more lengthy address needs further examination. Overgeneralized interpretation won't do. Instead, rightly dividing this text is in order!

> *Beware of the false prophets, who come to you in sheep's clothing, but inwardly are ravenous wolves. You will know them by their **fruits**. Grapes are not gathered from thorn bushes nor figs from thistles, are they? So every good tree bears good **fruit**, but the bad tree bears bad **fruit**. A good tree cannot produce bad **fruit**, nor can a bad tree produce good **fruit**. Every tree that does not bear good fruit is cut down and thrown into the fire. So then, you will know them by their **fruits*** **(Matthew 7:15-20).**

The first qualifying criteria Jesus gives after warning of false prophets is *fruit*. He says this is how we will recognize them. The inference here is that it will not be a mystery, a speculation, or even difficult to discern. Obviously, the crux then is in defining the word *fruit*. There's much to expound from these verses in defining the term, but the precision of one passage near the end of Jesus' address seems to leave no doubt as to how to define and recognize the fruit of these "false ones."

> *And then I will declare to them, "I never knew you; depart from Me, you who practice **lawlessness**." Therefore everyone who hears these words of Mine and acts on them, may be compared to a wise man who built his house on the rock. And the rain fell, and the floods came, and the winds*

blew and slammed against that house; and yet it did not fall, for it had been founded on the ***rock*** **(Matthew 7:23-25).**

Two qualifying words in this passage also help us to further define the fruit of the true from the false:

1. Lawlessness
2. Rock

Lawlessness is another way of saying "an unrepentant life-style of sinning." *Rock* is a metaphor for Jesus, as only those who build their house upon the Everlasting Rock (see Isa. 26:4) will survive the testing storms. It's important to also note in verse 23, Jesus says He will proclaim, "I *never* knew you." He didn't say, "I knew you, but you later turned sour." He didn't say, "I knew you, but you started walking in too much of the supernatural." He said *never.*

Jesus is in essence saying, "The false prophets I'm warning you about will make a regular and unrepentant practice of sin, because they will have not been truly born again. I will have never known them, they will not have built their house (life and ministry) upon Me, and their houses will be utterly cast down to prove it."

Interestingly, Jesus also said, "Many will *say* to Me on that day." He didn't say they'd actually perform miracles, but they'd merely claim to. Now, this may be a debatable matter, but the truth is we have no biblical record of a non-Christ follower performing miracles in Jesus' name. On the contrary, the seven sons of Sceva mentioned in Acts 19 were unsaved Jewish exorcists who once invoked Jesus' name in an attempt to cast out a devil but failed miserably. The demon responded, "Jesus I know, and Paul I've heard of, but who are you?" It then leaped on them and gave them such a beating they fled out of the house wounded and naked (see Acts 19:14-16)!

What Jesus also doesn't say is that "false prophets" will be supernatural ministers who walk with God, commit a sin, and face public judgment, but with repentance. If everyone who failed in the ministry were of the devil, we'd have to deem most all biblical figures as "false prophets" also. A perfect example would be King David, who walked with God, committed adultery, murdered a man to cover it up, and yet repented. God didn't condemn him as *false*. On the contrary, He still referred to him centuries later a man after His own heart (see Acts 13:22)!

Now, obviously the goal is to not heinously sin! Nevertheless, wisdom is rightly dividing those charlatans whom Jesus refers to in Matthew 7 who *never* knew Him, and those who knew Him but failed somewhere along the way. The latter are not to be deemed false prophets. On the contrary, they are to be prayed for and restored if possible (see Matt. 18:15; Gal. 6:1).

The *fruit* we should look for would then be a life revealing the opposite of lawlessness and sandy foundations. Now, no one in this life besides Jesus has ever perfectly fulfilled the Galatians 5 character fruits. However, long-term fruits such as love (see 1 Cor. 13:1-7; Gal. 5:22), peace, joy, and righteous living (see Phil. 1:11; Rom. 14:17) are a great indicator that a Jesus proclaimer is truly Jesus possessed.

In addition, Jesus said miraculous signs *would* follow true servants of Christ, and they'd include miracles, healings, deliverances, and more (see Mark 16:15-20; Heb. 2:4). The very purpose of signs, after all, is to point to something. Paul states that a person's faith in Christ should rest not on words only, but the demonstrative supernatural power of God (see 1 Cor. 2:4-6; 4:20; 1 Thess. 1:5)!

So, the miracles aren't the issue. Hearts and lifestyles are. Judge these things rightly, and we won't shy away from the very power of heaven meant to reveal it!

False Witnessing

The devil has a special hatred for people and places moving in the power of the Spirit, producing Christlike works (healing, deliverance, addiction breaking, peace, joy, etc.). Why? Because the anointing of the Holy Spirit breaks their bondage (see Isa. 10:27)!

> *How God anointed Jesus of Nazareth with the Holy Spirit and with power, and how He went about doing good and healing all who were under the tyranny of the Devil, because God was with Him* **(Acts 10:38 HCSB).**

The reader of this book is free to make his or her own judgments about its contents and the author. That is the prerogative of each, and I fully support it! Not only that, but I also genuinely love each one of you in the name of Christ. Even if we disagree or if you deem yourself my enemy, I still love you and bless you! Only I would advise caution in making judgments that are imprecise or contextually dishonest to the heart and facts of the principles and testimonies submitted. The Lord does not look kindly upon false witnessing. That goes for all of us. For there is no partiality with God (see Rom. 2:11).

> *And they stirred up the people, the elders and the scribes, and they came up to him and dragged him away and brought him before the Council. They put forward false witnesses* [against Stephen] **(Acts 6:12-13).**
>
> *For many were giving false testimony against Him* **(Mark 14:56).**
>
> *You shall not bear false witness against your neighbor* **(Exodus 20:16).**
>
> *A false witness will not go unpunished, and he who tells lies will perish* **(Proverbs 19:9).**

Conclusions

Discernment is not a vague, soulish feeling, but a holy, righteous judgment. We cannot just blanket the term *discernment* over everything we *feel* is uncomfortable. That would be foolish, as many times even in the Scripture people would at first be uncomfortable with God's ways. Some were even initially fearful of angels and/or manifestations of Jesus Himself. Hence their response, "Be not afraid" (see Luke 2:9-10; Rev. 1:17).

Again, the criteria for determining true from false spirits is biblically based. That is:

1. Does the person or spirit confess Jesus came in the flesh and as Lord? (See 1 John 4:1-3; 1 Corinthians 12:4-5.)
2. What name does the person or spirit come in or pray by—Jesus or otherwise? (See Mark 9:38-40; Acts 19:15.)
3. What (long-term) fruit does the person or spirit bear? (See Matthew 7:16; Philippians 1:11; John 15:7-8; Galatians 5:22-23.)

If a believer passes these three tests, they're not "false" according to the Scripture. They may disagree with you. They may even be wrong about some things, but they're not a heretic. A heretic is someone who denies Christ, His work, and exclusive divinity. A false witness is someone who slanders their Christian brother or sister based on generalizations and peripheral doctrinal disagreements.

> *If Satan also is divided against himself, how will his kingdom stand? For you say that I cast out demons by Beelzebul. And if I by Beelzebul cast out demons, by whom do your sons cast them out? So they will be your judges. But if I cast out demons by the finger of God, then the kingdom of God has come upon you* **(Luke 11:18-20).**

ABOUT JOSH ADKINS

Josh Adkins is the founder and senior pastor of Loft Church in Herrin, Illinois. His ministry is characterized by evangelistic passion, authenticity, humor, and a profound teaching gift, accompanied by uniquely powerful demonstrations of the Holy Spirit. Josh longs to see a world saved and a church scripturally equipped and miraculously empowered to reveal the God who is near!

For more information, please visit:

joshadkins.org

9:15AM

Song "Me ON your mind!